Multicurrency Mercantilism

The New International Monetary Order

Kathleen Tyson

6 October 2023

ISBN: 9798864645031

DEDICATION

For the Team and Advisors at Pacemaker.Global who
were the first to believe with me that better is possible, and
for my Followed and Followers on Twitter/X
who help me understand the changing world in real time.

CONTENTS

"When we talk about a global economy, and then use sanctions within the global economy, then the temptation will be that big countries thinking of their future will try to protect themselves against potential dangers, and as they do, they will create a mercantilist global economy."

Henry Kissinger, 2014

"The more we condition the use of the dollar and our financial system on adherence to US foreign policy, the more the risk of migration to other currencies and other financial systems in the medium-term grows."

Jack Lew, 2016

"If you weaponize currency enough times, other countries will stop using it."

Elon Musk, 2023

1 MULTICURRENCY MERCANTILISM

Before titling this book, I searched Google for 'Multicurrency Mercantilism'. The search had zero hits.

That any two-word search in the English language yields zero hits surprises in 2023. It shows how unfashionable mercantilism has become after 80 years of global dollar dominance and US hegemony.

Mercantilism is generally understood as exporting more than is imported to accumulate national wealth, formerly as gold and silver, but today I would add official sector currency reserves, alternative marketable assets, and equity stakes in foreign industry and infrastructure. Mercantilists aim to growth national wealth; capitalists aim to grow increasingly stateless and untaxed private profits and private wealth. Capitalism has dominated the last century; mercantilism may dominate the next century. This book is about the transition now clearly in progress.

Multicurrency Mercantilism as a description of the new monetary order comes from a Henry Kissinger observation in 2014:

> "When we talk about a global economy, and then use sanctions within the global economy, then the temptation will be that big countries thinking of their future will try to protect themselves against potential dangers, and as they do, they will create a mercantilist global economy."

Kissinger was right. In 2023 we have mercantilist nations transacting in more diverse currencies and more diverse assets than the 2022 dollarised global economy. Dollar's eighty-year dominance in the world is waning as the share of trade, credit, and investment in mercantilist currencies increases. As more states experiment with Multicurrency Mercantilism the transition will accelerate.

Excessive Western sovereign debt and monetary laxity have contributed to unease among mercantilist states from 2009, but the decisive shift to Monetary Mercantilism in 2023 has been motivated by sanctions. The US and its allies over-used sanctions, driving the rest of the world to defensive trade in alternative currencies.

Financial and economic sanctions now apply to 30% of global GDP with more than 12,000 sanctions against Russia. US and allied commercial sanctions in telecommunications, microchips, and advanced technologies against China, the top trading partner of 120 nations are also driving mercantilist policies. Destabilising Chinese industry presents a critical risk for most of the world's economies, particularly those who ship primary resources to China's massive industrial sector or depend on China for their electricity, telecommunications, and other civil infrastructure. 2022 drove many states to recalibrate national security priorities to protect financial sectors, supply chains, and civil infrastructure from sanctions.

Sanctions use has broadened rapidly. Economic sanctions used to target the banking sector, limiting access to dollar settlements, but over the last five years they expanded more widely to commercial and technology operations and the payment network Swift. Multicurrency Mercantilism is now global economic, financial and commercial self-defence.

Sanctions Programs and Country Information

OFAC administers a number of different sanctions programs. The sanctions can be either comprehensive or selective, using the blocking of assets and trade restrictions to accomplish foreign policy and national security goals.

WHERE IS OFAC'S COUNTRY LIST?

Q   Filter by program name

Sanctions Programs and Country Information

Active Sanctions Programs	Program Last Updated
Afghanistan-Related Sanctions	Feb 25, 2022
Balkans-Related Sanctions	Jul 31, 2023
Belarus Sanctions	Aug 09, 2023
Burma-Related Sanctions	Sep 25, 2023
Central African Republic Sanctions	Jan 20, 2023
Chinese Military Companies Sanctions	Jun 01, 2022
Counter Narcotics Trafficking Sanctions	Oct 03, 2023
Counter Terrorism Sanctions	Sep 27, 2023
Countering America's Adversaries Through Sanctions Act-Related Sanctions	Sep 14, 2023
Cuba Sanctions	Sep 26, 2022
Cyber-Related Sanctions	Sep 18, 2023
Democratic Republic of the Congo-Related Sanctions	Aug 24, 2023
Ethiopia-Related Sanctions	Feb 08, 2023
Foreign Interference in a United States Election Sanctions	Mar 03, 2022
Global Magnitsky Sanctions	Aug 24, 2023
Hong Kong-Related Sanctions	Dec 20, 2021
Hostages and Wrongfully Detained U.S. Nationals Sanctions	Sep 18, 2023
Iran Sanctions	Sep 27, 2023
Iraq-Related Sanctions	Aug 23, 2023
Lebanon-Related Sanctions	Aug 10, 2023
Libya Sanctions	Oct 17, 2022
Magnitsky Sanctions	Aug 17, 2023
Mali-Related Sanctions	Aug 04, 2023
Nicaragua-related Sanctions	Apr 19, 2023
Non-Proliferation Sanctions	Sep 27, 2023
North Korea Sanctions	Aug 31, 2023
Rough Diamond Trade Controls	Jun 18, 2018
Russian Harmful Foreign Activities Sanctions	Oct 12, 2023
Somalia Sanctions	May 24, 2023
South Sudan-Related Sanctions	Jun 20, 2023
Sudan and Darfur Sanctions	Sep 26, 2023
Syria Sanctions	Sep 18, 2023
Syria-Related Sanctions (Executive Order 13894 of 2019)	Aug 17, 2023
Transnational Criminal Organizations	Jun 16, 2023
Ukraine-/Russia-related Sanctions	Sep 14, 2023
Venezuela-Related Sanctions	Jul 28, 2023
Yemen-related Sanctions	Nov 18, 2021
Zimbabwe Sanctions	Dec 12, 2022

Information on OFAC sanctions lists program tags and their definitions.

Multicurrency Mercantilism protects states and their non-state actors from future sanctions, targeted economic destabilisations, and interrupted commerce. Most of the world chooses trade and cooperation with Russia, China, and other sanctioned states such as Venezuela, Cuba, Syria, and Iran. States in the global East and South now actively agree and plan to shift from dollar invoicing to Local Currency Trade (LCT) in alternative currencies as a pragmatic response to the risks in Western sovereign debt as monetary reserves and the parallel risks of sanctions.

Zero hits on Google validates originality for Multicurrency Mercantilism, but also highlights the urgent need for an explanation, however incomplete, of the new monetary order now emerging.

This book is not an economics essay with complicated models. It is not a comprehensive history on the rights and wrongs of how we got to where we are. This book is a practical guide, written at speed as events unfold, describing likely changes in the global monetary order and global economy. It offers optimism about a better, more stable, more equitable future monetary order if we collectively get this transition right. The transition can be gradual, manageable, and win-win for everyone, even Americans.

The chapters that follow illustrate the main features of Multicurrency Mercantilism:

- **The alternative to the dollar *is* the dollar and *ALL* other currencies.** Everyone accepting dollars for international trade was the norm to 2022. Now more state and non-state actors prefer other currencies, either their own or regional currencies. The dollar will retain pre-eminence as the sole hegemonic currency, but other currencies are gaining in trade and credit. For example, India first paid for Russian oil in 2022 in dollars, then Russian rubles, then Indian rupees, then United Arab Emirates dirhams, then Chinese yuan. It's all good money if the parties to a deal agree a currency for payment. Using alternative currencies requires no new treaties, laws, regulations, or official authorisation. Choice of currency is a private commercial matter. We all have a right to choose any currency in negotiating each cross-border contract or credit – and a right to change our minds too. Reference prices will continue in dollars for many commodities even as payment shifts to alternatives.

- **The transition to Multicurrency Mercantilism will be gradual**. Using more currencies should not be destabilising unless policymakers overreact, or war widens from Ukraine to Asia. Global trade in goods is approximately $46 trillion annually, approximately half in dollars in 2023, so $23 trillion can still move to rival currencies. This is modest compared to global finance in bonds (over $307 trillion par value), equities (over $108 trillion market capitalisation), derivatives ($635 trillion notional value), and foreign exchange (about $1,900 trillion annual settlements). Capital markets will continue to be dollar dominated because the dollar dominates all these financial instruments. Market settlements and margin flows in dollars will still vastly exceed the modest $23 trillion in non-dollar global goods trade. If half of that $23 trillion shifts to LCT over five years, that is just $11.5 trillion in export payments. The G7 should hardly notice. The challenges for stability in global financial market are not going to come from Local Currency Trade in exports; the challenges will come from the internal dysfunction of bond, credit, and derivatives markets.

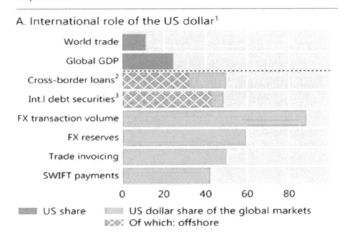

The international role of the US dollar

In per cent

A. International role of the US dollar[1]

Source: Maronoti, B., Revisiting the International Role of the US Dollar, *BIS Quarterly Review* (December 2022), https://www.bis.org/publ/qtrpdf/r_qt2212x.htm

- **No new hegemon** will challenge the US. Being a hegemon requires a capacity for military, political, and clandestine violence to punish and destabilise leaders and states that do not align with your currency or foreign policies. An attempted coup in Kazakhstan in January 2022 and successful coup in Pakistan in April 2022 illustrate the risks of non-alignment with US policies. Blowing up the Nordstream pipelines was a hegemonic discipline against Europe and the euro. Multicurrency Mercantilism does not require a hegemon as no currency claims primacy and all currencies are eligible alternatives. No one will compel decisions around the world by millions of state and non-state actors, through billions of diverse contracts and agreements, each electing alternative currencies for trade. China is the world's top trading partner to 120 countries, so Chinese yuan makes commercial sense for many trades, and China promotes the use of yuan as official policy. Nonetheless, the choice whether to use dollar, yuan, or another currency is for states, corporations, creditors, and customers. China doesn't force yuan use, and is unlikely to bomb, invade, occupy, assassinate, coup, sanction, or destabilise those who don't choose yuan.

Bigger driver
Asia will contribute about 70% of global growth this year.

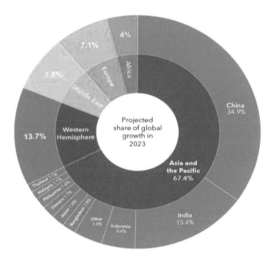

Source: IMF, World Economic Outlook, April 2023.
Note: Groupings based on IMF Regional Economic Outlook classifications.

IMF

- **Globalisation will accelerate**. While the West talks of de-coupling or de-risking dependence on Russia and China, global economic interdependence and supply chains are irreversible. Globalisation now accelerates as China shares world-beating energy and transport infrastructure, telecommunications, technologies, industrial scale, logistics, and governance principles with the global East and South. Western corporations must also seek profit from global growth opportunities or fade to unprofitability and irrelevance. Multicurrency Mercantilism also re-integrates the 30% of global GDP in countries currently sanctioned and cut off from dollar systems. Iran, Syria, Venezuela, and Russia prove currency optionality is possible, practical, and profitable.

- **The Angell Paradox: Sanctions devalue contracts, assets, and claims of the sanctioners with the sanctioned.** 1932 Nobel Peace Prize recipient Sir Norman Angell observed in *The Great Illusion* that economic sanctions between interdependent developed economies at war always impoverish the sanctioner as well as the sanctioned. No one 'wins' a sanctions war. Freezes, seizures, expropriations, repudiation of contracts and debts, and denial of access to banks and payment systems all devalue the Wests assets, markets, rule of law, and infrastructure. The dollar's share of official reserves fell at its fastest rate in 2022 as central banks globally shunned US Treasuries for the security of gold in self-custody. US Treasuries have fallen in value for three years in a row, a new record. Sanctions blowback for commercial and technology sanctions on China are even more remarkable. Exports fell sharply for technology and chip industries in US itself, but also in Japan, Korea, Taiwan, and the Netherlands after those states joined technology sanctions against China. Sanctions now impair company valuations, profitability, future investment, and research and development. Meanwhile Chinese technology companies overcame supply chain shocks at record speed and are regaining dominance. The UN Charter discourages unilateral sanctions, as do the BRICS (Brazil, Russia, India, China, South Africa.), and rightly so.

 Olalatech 🌐 🏴
@olalatech1

The scariest thing in business is a company losing everything... and then they rise up against their enemies...

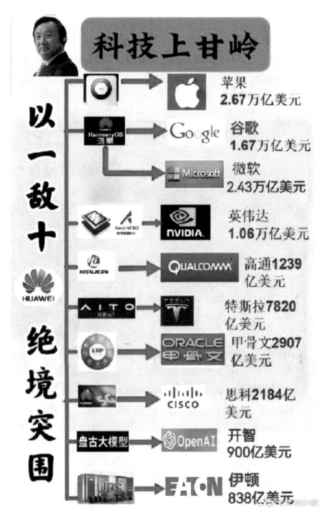

- **Multicurrency Mercantilism will improve resiliency, stability, and inflation.** The dollar has always been a vector of systemic risk, instability, and inflation within the US itself and to others globally. Economic shocks, interest rate hikes, and liquidity shortages always hurt vulnerable economies first and most, and these recover more slowly too. As countries use their own currencies for trade and longer-term, bilateral co-development projects, they can achieve much better stability, resilience, and lower inflation. Central bank policies in rivals Russia and China also foster superior price stability, so emulation of their policies may have wider benefit.

- **Gold is back as a hegemonic asset.** Gold held primacy as a hegemonic asset for interstate settlements, tribute, and war reparations from antiquity to 1971. Gold resumed a role in official reserves after 2008 and became the dominant reserve for central bank accumulation in 2022. There have been calls for a global synthetic currency blending foreign exchange and commodities, but there is no material progress. Any formula, governance, logistics, and auditing are complicated and challenging, potentially gamed. Quite plainly, gold is what we can agree now.

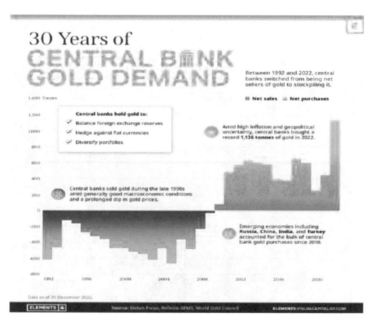

- **Technology will speed and de-risk the Multicurrency Mercantilism transition**. Cloud, internet, telecommunications, financial data standards, agile methodology, and banking technologies provide reliable, secure, repeatable, cost effective, scalable solutions for diverse currencies.

Code once, download and API to reach many. The same infrastructure and data interchange standards that globalised dollars and euros can be adapted for all other currencies. Global commercial banks already maintain multicurrency ledgers, so why not governments and businesses too? Once the choice is made, the means is available. Anyone can have multicurrency payments and investments in 2023.

- **Debt is the biggest stability challenge**. Exactly how Multicurrency Mercantilism will impact the vast $307 trillion markets for sovereign, financial sector, corporate, and consumer debt is difficult to project. Nations that migrate to LCT for trade will no longer be motivated to accumulate Western sovereign debt as foreign exchange reserves. Official foreign exchange reserves peaked in 2021. Rapid rate hikes in 2022-23 have devalued benchmark 10-year US Treasury more than 25%, a 20-year US Treasury more than 35%. In Europe's bond markets the losses are even worse, averaging 50%, as Europe started raising rates from a decade of negative rates. Massive losses on bond portfolios have destabilised central banks, banks, pension funds, insurance companies, and asset managers. Systemic illiquidity and market dysfunction remain a perpetual risk. Higher interest rates are particularly destabilising to EMDEs, hurting the poorest the most. Stabilising bond and debt markets is a global challenge that requires renewed commitment to collaboration among all economic stakeholders. Fiscal discipline, long absent in Western politics, will have to return as domestic capacity for absorbing more bonds reaches a limit.

- **Better is possible**. When the US imposed Bretton Woods Accords on its wartime allies in 1944 it held

80% of world gold, 50% of global GDP, and a monopoly on the global projection of military power. The dollar order was a security-military order that promised security to those who aligned with the dollar and projected force against those who resisted dollar dominance. The US led the post-war order with the United Nations in New York, the IMF and World Bank in Washington, and its military deployed to more than 800 bases globally. The emerging order is an economic cooperation order without leadership or enforcement, dynamically adapting as states share successful methods more widely. If global growth accelerates and stabilises, we all win.

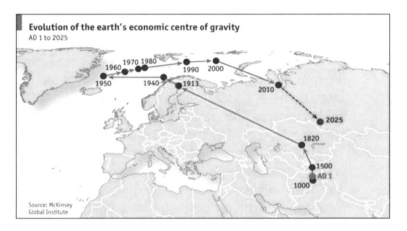

Why do I care about Multicurrency Mercantilism enough to write this book? I am a 'plumber' of global financial payments, settlements, and liquidity. The transition from the dollarised world to Multicurrency Mercantilism fascinates me and I want to build any new plumbing it needs to make the transition safer and use of more currencies practical and resilient.

I started as a central banker at the Federal Reserve Bank of

New York with early responsibility for financial stability, systemic risk, and explaining payment and settlement systems' interdependencies and vulnerabilities. I went on to build much of the capital markets infrastructure in London and Luxembourg that dollarised, grew, connected, and harmonised global capital markets. I globalised liquidity in US Treasuries by gaining a ground-breaking authorisation to clear and settle Treasuries in the Clearstream depository in Luxembourg. I wrote the first Triparty Repo to create an interbank secured credit market averaging $18 trillion in daily secured credit. Foreign exchange averaged $930 billion a day when I designed foreign exchange settlement operations for the founders of Continuous Linked Settlement. CLS Bank now settles an average $7.5 trillion a day in 18 currencies, and peak $14 trillion a day. Swift's Market Infrastructure Resiliency Service was my idea. I then standardised the Reserve Bank of India fully modern, real-time, integrated operating platform to 14 central banks globally. I have always been passionate about making the world's markets more efficient, safer, better, and that passion is undimmed today.

Good infrastructure grows markets. Multicurrency Mercantilism will require some new infrastructure and 'plumbing' to reach all currencies and mitigate risks of greater global complexity. States, central banks, bank consortia, clearinghouses, payment platforms, and settlement systems will all have to adapt to a new reality.

My last book had 3,400 painfully conformed academic citations. This one doesn't use academic citations as anything published in journals is already 2-3 years behind events. Instead, I'm trying something new: dropping in illustrations or observations from Twitter/X. I've built a community of interest in Multipolar transition there as @Kathleen_Tyson_. Collectively we share more objective analysis of global events in real time and get immediate, expert feedback and correction. Subscription media I follow is too often behind trends or biased and partial in their coverage. X is invaluable in times of rapid change. Thanks, @elonmusk!

 Aly-Khan Satchu @alykhansatchu · 1h
people in China and the non-Western world must realize that when it comes to the workings of the mainstream media we are in a new era – a propaganda war the likes of which the world has never seen before, powered by today's digital technology.

thediplomat.com
Anti-China Rhetoric Is Off the Charts in Western Media

 Elon Musk ☑ ✖ @elonmusk · 10h
I don't read the legacy media propaganda much anymore. It's a waste of time and a sadness generator.

Just get my news from X – much more immediate, has actual world-class subject matter experts and tons of humor.

Sooo much better!

○ 14K   ⟲ 30K   ♡ 204K   ⅱ 10.8M   ⬆

This book has been composed at speed to document momentous change. It is meant to be helpful, not dispositive. No doubt I'll revise it periodically, perhaps annually, as events, policies, data emerge. I will put a publication date on the title page for each iteration. Today's date is 6 October 2023. No doubt momentous change will come tomorrow, next week, next month, but I must hit the Publish button sometime, and it is today.

In case you were wondering, no AI was used in writing.

2 DOLLAR ALTERNATIVES

Many people, even quite sophisticated financial professionals, find Multicurrency Mercantilism unimaginable because dealing in dollars is so widespread after 80 years of dollar dominance. All major  corporations, investors, banks, and traders already use dollars. Many individual savers around the world prefer a stack of dollars to domestic currencies for savings. Banks add hefty foreign exchange fees and interest premia for services in all but the largest alternative currencies, penalising use of anything but dollars.

This tiered and discriminatory system is now openly challenged. More than 80 countries have announced policies favouring use of local or rival currencies. All major corporations, investors, banks, traders, and even individuals can already use all major and many minor currencies for trade in goods and services. In 2022 Singapore, India, Iran,

Russia, China, and Brazil opened domestic payment platforms to foreign banks, eliminating the high costs of Swift messaging and interbank foreign exchange trades for global use of their currencies. The cost and complexity of shifting more payments to alternative currencies is falling rapidly as collective expertise, systems, and methods are shared worldwide.

Sasha Breger Bush ✓
@IPEwithSBB   ···

The #dollar is in serious trouble. "[M]ore than 80 countries [are] currently engaged in de-dollarization planning and implementation via multilateral organizations." And this is only one of many strategies currently being deployed by members of the international movement against the #USD.

dollarsandsense.org/archives/2023/...

Multilateral Organizations Pursuing De-Dollarization Plans	
Organization	**Members**
BRICS	Brazil, Russia, India, China, South Africa
Mercosur	Argentina, Brazil, Paraguay, Uruguay
SCO	China, India, Kazakhstan, Kyrgyzstan, Russia, Pakistan, Tajikistan, Uzbekistan
EEU	Armenia, Belarus, Kazakhstan, Kyrgyzstan, Russia
ASEAN	Brunei, Cambodia, Indonesia, Laos, Malaysia, Myanmar, the Philippines, Singapore, Thailand, Vietnam
African Union (AU)	Algeria, Angola, Benin, Botswana, Burkina Faso, Burundi, Cameroon, Cabo Verde, CAR, Chad, Comoros, Congo, Côte d'Ivoire, Djibouti, DRC, Egypt, Equatorial Guinea, Eritrea, Kingdom of Eswatini, Ethiopia, Gabon, Gambia, Ghana, Guinea, Guinea-Bissau, Kenya, Lesotho, Liberia, Libya, Madagascar, Malawi, Mali, Mauritania, Mauritius, Morocco, Mozambique, Namibia, Niger, Nigeria, Uganda, Rwanda, SADR, Sao Tome and Principe, Senegal, Seychelles, Sierra Leone, Somalia, South Africa, South Sudan, Sudan, Tanzania, Togo, Tunisia, Zambia, Zimbabwe

Even Small and Medium Enterprises (SMEs) and individuals can now be multicurrency: PayPal (25 currencies), Wise (21 currencies), WeChat Pay (16 currencies), and Alipay (14 currencies) already make cross-border multicurrency invoicing, credit, and payments easy to contract and manage. This is great for a world where global banks have underserved SMEs, supressing the most dynamic part of any economy for growth and employment.

Currency hegemony rarely lasts more than a century. Dollar dominance appears to be fading in sequence with other hegemons more or less to schedule. Dollar dominance started with the innovation of official foreign exchange reserves in the Genoa Convention of 1922 and ended with the reversion to gold as the preferred hegemonic asset in 2022. As dominant currency, the dollar benefitted disproportionately from foreign accumulation of dollar balances and assets. Multicurrency Mercantilism ends this subsidy, but perhaps without immediate impact.

Reserve Currency Colonialism

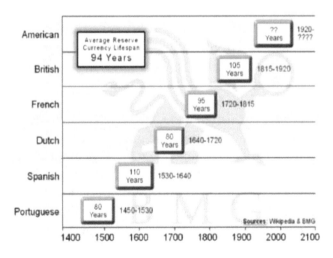

If a critical mass of the global economy were to shift from dollars, wouldn't they agree on a single alternative? Apparently not. Looking at events over the past two years, state and non-state actors are taking diverse and uncoordinated decisions with their trading partners and customers as they shift to alternative currencies. State and non-state contracting parties have diverse interests and capacities in alternative currencies, different costs, and varied access to swaps, banks, and payment platforms. They rationally and pragmatically make diverse choices.

As each actor makes choices suited to their own interests and capacities, we can be optimistic that multicurrency optionality is good for the world. Local Currency Trade has many advantages relative to dollar dominance or any single alternative.

- LCT does not require consent of the G7 nations that dominate the Bretton Woods II monetary order and cannot be vetoed by them. The choice of currency for contract or credit is strictly a matter for the contracting parties and can be kept commercially confidential if they so choose. This allows the transition to happen quietly, dynamically, quickly, and mostly unobserved. Local payment systems volumes are not aggregated for statistical tracking yet.

- Alternative currencies require no new treaties, laws, regulations, or multilateral infrastructure. Any two parties can agree a currency for settlement. So long as the bank or payment platform acts on their instruction, commerce can shift immediately to alternative currencies. Sanctions may limit the scope of Western bank or platform participation, but do not affect acts of other banks or payment platforms. There truly is global optionality now, freedom to choose.

- Interbank domestic payments systems are already proven secure and reliable. While interlinking payment systems may be useful, it isn't essential. Modernisation of payments systems to promote wider access, multicurrency clearing, and interoperability will increase access and optionality.

- LCT can provide superior transparency on exports and commercial proceeds. Pricing exports in their own currencies helps states identify revenues and collect corporate taxes and customs tariffs. In this way LCT can expand fiscal capacity for exporters. For too long dollarised trade, particularly in energy or food, has been dominated by a handful of ill-transparent brokers who use tax havens and suppress export levies. Dominant energy traders Vitol, Valero, and Trafigura were cut out of Russian energy exports in 2022 and ruble pricing imposed for 'unfriendly' countries. Russia observed greatly increased revenues and export levies that improved Russian state fiscal capacity. Others can study whether export pricing in own currency will have similar benefit. Increasing fiscal capacity means improvements to education, healthcare, and infrastructure, and so future growth and stability.

- LCT can be implemented incrementally as each nation, bank or corporation adapts its contractual, accounting, invoicing, and financial framework to more currencies and evaluates the benefits. Nations can experiment with LCT in one or two export commodities to assess the results and then expand

LCT according to identified benefits.

- LCT may improve debt service capacity by making export revenues more predictable and less prone to exchange rate volatility. Paying foreign debt in dollars rendered countries vulnerable to shocks, tighter credit, or liquidity shortages. As the dollar strengthened in 2022, and global credit became constrained, ever more countries explored LCT as a way to insulate their economies from dollar vulnerability.

- LCT may improve domestic planning. Export and import relationships are relatively stable and predictable (except weather impact on crop yields, strikes, etc). All countries measure their principal exports and imports. Policy makers can make plans with trading partners for investments and trade credit avoiding dollar volatility and liquidity risks. The WTO Bilateral Import data provides a useful resource to explore and prioritise each country's most important export/import partners for transition planning and prioritisation.

- Credit ratings for the state, financial sector, and non-financial sector could also improve, lowering debt service burdens and widening access to global credit. The cost of dollar finance in many EMDEs is multiples of the cost of finance in the G7. Narrowing the spread should be a policy aim of LCT.

- LCT can eliminate the overhead of KYC-AML-CTF. Commercial bank trade finance capacity has steadily contracted as many commercial banks withdrew from the low margin sector. Aggressive fines in the billions by US Treasury and other authorities discouraged banks from dealing with all but the largest and most profitable clients, leaving small and medium exporters locked out of the global economy. LCT through local banks will reduce compliance risks, red tape, foreign exchange risks, hedging costs, and cross-border banking complexity. The high spreads charged by banks in foreign exchange can be narrowed by using local or linked currencies, growing SMEs and making global trade and commerce more equitable.

- LCT reduces the risk of unilateral sanctions disrupting trade. A 2018 paper in the medical journal *The Lancet* was titled *Economic Sanction: A weapon of Mass Destruction*. It explained how economic sanctions affect the health of populations and devastate economies, as tragically evident today in Venezuela, Syria, and Yemen. LCT in partner currencies will reduce the social harms of sanctions and stabilise countries targeted for destabilisation.

- LCT can reduce inequality and exploitation. Exporting energy, minerals, and commodities in dollar tends to undervalue domestic production and labour. Local pricing of export commodities can promote higher real wages, lower credit costs, increase local consumption, encourage investment, secure fiscal capacity, and so reduce global income and wealth inequalities.

- Finally, there is no need for complicated or expensive new financial infrastructure or a new global currency to replace the dollar. Every currency is eligible. It is up to the parties to any trade to choose the currency or currencies that suit their interests. They can even choose electricity, gold, or oil for payment. As we saw in 2022, countries can adapt existing payment systems, domestic bank operations, corporate accounting, and central bank operations in weeks or months rather than years.

LCT is progressing everywhere. LCT was agreed at regional level among the Association of South East Asian Nations (ASEAN) unanimously at ASEAN's May 2023 meeting in Indonesia. ASEAN central banks are working together to interlink national interbank and even retail payment platforms to LCT for regional imports, exports, and tourism.

Multicurrency Mercantilism implies the end of the 50-year petrodollar monopoly on global energy trade. The Petrodollar started 2022 secure, but by mid-2023 oil and gas were trading for dollars, euros, yen, yuan, dirham, rupee, and bartered for gold, airport constuction, and electricity. As oil and gas trades are not uniformly reported, there may be other currencies or barters buying energy as well. Russia inspired other energy exporters to experiment. What had seemed unimaginable for energy dealers in 2021 proved practical in 2022, and pragmatic in 2023.

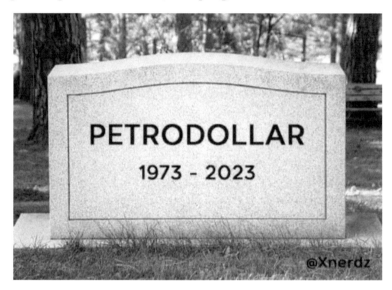

On 9 December 2022 President Xi invited the Gulf Cooperation Council heads of state to sell oil to China through the Shanghai Petroleum and Natural Gas Exchange in yuan. Bilateral cooperation also expanded to hydrogen energy, energy storage, smart electrical networks, and nuclear energy. The first UAE shipment of natural gas for yuan followed in March 2023. The solidarity of seven heads of the GCC states coming to Riyadh to stand united with their largest customer showed collective determination for change, opening a new era. American envoys travelled

to Beijing and Riyadh to try to undo the decision, but their efforts to reinforce the petrodollar failed.

Few beyond Washington and New York will regred the end of the Petrodollar era. It was violent and brutal as the US military enforced dollar use against those who strayed. Iraq, Libya, and Syria remain devastated warzones where they once were the most prosperous regional states.

Announcements of bilateral LCT are almost daily now: Brazil and Argentina will trade in yuan, Bolivia and China will trade in bolivar and yuan, Bangladesh and India will trade in taka and rupee, UAE and India will trade in dirham and rupee. Bilateral progress is dynamic, rapid and unstoppable.

Different countries can take different routes to the LCT transition. Reserve Bank of India's remarkable success in globalising rupee started with central bank operational modernisation in 2012. RBI has now opened vostro accounts for 20 peer central banks and 40 global commercial banks in 2022-23, enabling access to rupee settlements.

The RBI transformation is one of the most significant technology achievements. I was so impressed at the speed, the scale, with no loss of data and no interruption of operations, I worked with Intellect, the supplier, to standardise and globalise the platform. The resulting fully integrated platform (with real time balance sheet visibility) now runs 14 central banks, including at least one multicurrency implementation. The Unified Payments Interface (UPI) combines interbank, digital, and mobile payments. UPI enabled withdrawal of high value currency notes in India to crack down on tax avoidance. In April 2023, UPI transactions reached 8.9 billion, with a total transaction value of INR 14.07 trillion (USD 168.9 billion). This was a 59 percent increase in UPI transactions and a 49 percent growth in transaction value year on year from April 2022. 30 peer central banks now have vostro accounts for payments in rupees.

 China – Arab Forum (CAF) – المنتدى العربي الصيني @china_arabia · Aug 18 ⋯
🇨🇳 🌍 China's outbound direct investment in **BRI** nations up 15% to $12bln in H1 **2023**

zawya.com
China's outbound direct investment in BRI nations up 15% to $12bln i...
The value of total overseas M&A deals falls to $11.7bln, says E&Y report

💬   🔁 1   ♡ 1   ⁂ 258   ⬆

China uses bilateral diplomacy, infrastructure construction, credit finance, and trade for global influence. Parallel to its Belt and Road Initiative, Peoples' Bank of China negotiated bilateral swap lines in yuan with a wide network of more than 30 central banks and set up branches of its export banks abroad. The China Interbank Payment System (CIPS) processed CNY 96.7 trillion (USD 14.03 trillion) in payments in 2022 between 1427 financial institutions in 109 countries. Yuan swap lines make it easy for banks in a distant capital to service infrastructure loans or borrow trade finance in yuan, knowing that exports to China, the biggest trade partner for 120 states, will securely fund repayment. Yuan gained significant traction from 2010 to 2021, and the pace accelerated sharply in 2022 and into 2023. More recently Argentina has twice drawn on its yuan swap line to make payments on its debts to the International Monetary Fund, reducing dependence on dollar reserves for debt servicing.

Published academic research on yuan swap lines and trade is too often flawed by reliance on data from Swift's RMB Tracker. Many countries now have direct access to yuan through CIPS, Chinese trade bank branches in their countries, and Chinese commercial platforms such as

AliPay or WeChatPay. None of these cross-border payment channels are aggregated by Swift. BIS and scholarly research on cross-border payment and credit flows using Swift data understates RMB use and is now misleading.

Unlike Western central bank swaps, innovated to stabilise financial markets short of liquidity, China's swap lines are explicitly mercantile. Western swaps are not meant to provide funding beyond the financial sector, but China's swap lines are meant to reach every sector of receiving country economies. 2023 saw record use of RMB swap lines, reaching a reported 120 billion yuan, about $17 billion dollars. Confidence in yuan finance gives corporates and exporters confidence to expand investment and production. Yuan swaps reduce both sides' risk of trade disruption from sanctions, and so improve bilateral economic security and resiliency.

Figure 1   China FX currency swap agreement illustration from an importer perspective in Egypt

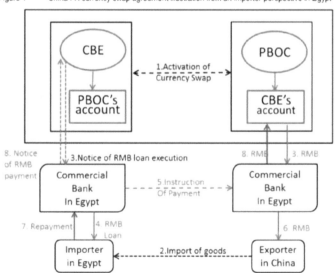

Source: The Treatment of Currency Swaps between Central Banks: Egypt Experience (the Central Bank of Egypt, 2017)

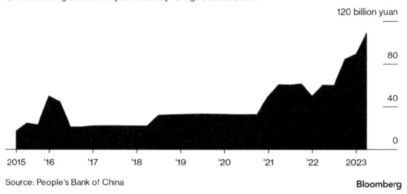

Global Central Banks' Use of PBOC Swap Lines at A Record
Foreign countries increasingly tapped currency swap to get yuan

■ Outstanding balance of yuan used by foreign central banks

120 billion yuan

80

40

0

2015   '16   '17   '18   '19   '20   '21   '22   2023

Source: People's Bank of China

Bloomberg

Russia appears to have a different strategy for global engagement, with more focus on the Middle East and Africa. Primary resources align with Russia's own strength as a global storehouse of minerals and energy, as well as a major agricultural exporter. Russia has long collaborated with OPEC states on oil and gas market stability and pricing. In 2022 Russia intensified its diplomacy with OPEC. The 2023 focus has shifted to Africa where Russia has always promoted independence and de-colonising, as well as greater African influence in global institutions. The Russia-Africa Summit 2023 ended with several states seeking Russian cooperation on internal security to remove foreign occupations and terrorists while improving resource and energy production.

Much attention has been focused on the BRICS+ intentions for monetary and economic cooperation. A BRICS currency has been discussed as a potential rival to the dollar for over a decade. Scepticism is warranted: synthetic and basket currencies always end up gamed by select participants. For example, the latest reweighting of the IMF Special Drawing Rights quietly abandoned the export-weighted formula agreed in 2014 to keep GBP as a component, rather than cede another Western currency's place in the SDR to an Asian currency. A gold-redeemable BRICS currency might have advantages as a trade currency and non-inflationary reserve, but the governance, logistics, trust, custody, audit, assay, and redemption challenges are daunting. As with the gold-backed dollar under both the Federal Reserve and Bretton Woods, a BRICS gold-backed currency could be undermined and destabilised by redemptions even if reserves of deliverable gold are ample. It's worth remembering that the dollar started as 100% gold reserve, was diminished in 1917 to 40% reserve, diminished again in 1933 to $35 per ounce of gold, and removed entirely from the gold standard in 1971. Gold alone is no defence from monetary debasement.

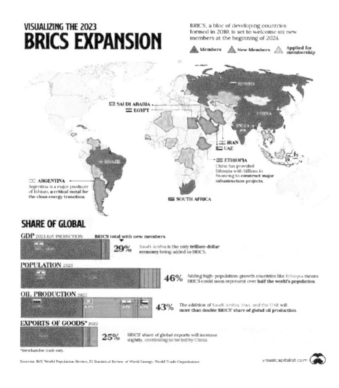

The best policy of BRICS+ may be constructive ambiguity. As long as the US and its allies are distracted watching for a long-mooted BRICS+ currency, they might miss the interconnection of domestic currency payments and credit happening at speed in the background.

A major open issue is what happens to currencies pegged to the dollar or euro? States that took a decision to peg will need to re-evaluate, if they are not already, whether there is still an advantage in being pegged to USD. Below are some of the standard rationales for pegging and why review is timely.

- **Stability:** Pegs promote stability because the fixed rate of conversion to a dominant currency builds greater public confidence. As the dollar and US Treasuries become less stable, instability may be communicated through pegs.

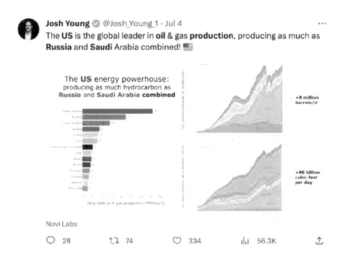

- **Trade:** Oil exporters adopted dollar pegs because oil priced in petrodollars and US was the biggest client before the shale boom. Now US is the largest global oil exporter and a rival to most peg states. Most OPEC oil ships to Asia, with China the top client. A dollar peg will be less aligned with post-petrodollar trade.

- **Reserves alignment:** Pegged states tend to accumulate official reserves in the dominant currency. Rapid devaluation of US Treasuries as rates rose in 2022-23 was not good for stability or alignment. The value of benchmark Treasuries has fallen three years in a row.

Major Fixed Currencies

Country	Region	Currency Name	Code	Peg Rate	Rate Since
Bahrain	Middle East	Dinar	BHD	0.38	2018
Belize	Central America	Dollar	BZ$	2.00	1978
Cuba	Central America	Convertible Peso	CUC	1.000	2011
Djibouti	Africa	Franc	DJF	177.721	1973
Eritrea	Africa	Nakfa	ERN	15.07	2018
Hong Kong	Asia	Dollar	HKD	7.76	2020
Jordan	Middle East	Dinar	JOD	0.71	1995
Lebanon	Middle East	Pound	LBP	1507.5	1997
Oman	Middle East	Rial	OMR	0.385	1986
Panama	Central America	Balboa	PAB	1.000	1904
Qatar	Middle East	Riyal	QAR	3.64	2001
Saudi Arabia	Middle East	Riyal	SAR	3.75	2003
United Arab Emirates	Middle East	Dirham	AED	3.673	1997

Source: The World Bank

Godfree Roberts ✅
@GodfreeTrh   ...

Gavekal Economics: "Since the start of Covid, long-dated Chinese
government bonds have outperformed long-dated US treasuries by
35%!
"In fact, Chinese bonds have been a beacon of stability.
You can look at recent market behavior and conclude that as Chinese
banks have spent the last year outperforming US treasuries, the
immediate problem is not in the Chinese financial system, but in the US
treasury market itself.
**"If so, we are entering a new world in which US treasuries can no
longer be thought of as the bedrock on which to build portfolios".**

tinyurl.com/4p6cpvz2Want

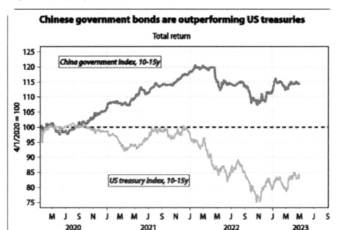

11:40 AM · Aug 25, 2023 · **9,275** Views

- **Lack of skills/capacity:** States tend to peg in a crisis or
  when domestic governance is questioned, but as states
  mature and improve domestic governance, education,
  skills, expertise, and capacity, most can resume
  management of their currency without a peg. The
  recent Fitch downgrade of US Treasuries explicitly
  challenged US fiscal and governance capacity, which
  should worry pegged currency states.

- **Rates:** Rates policies of peg countries are constrained by US rates, and so pegged central banks must raise rates in parallel with Federal Reserve or risk destabilising the peg. Now that many pegged economies are mature and diversified, and generally quite different in character than the government and consumer debt dominated US economy, they might well benefit from different monetary and rates policies than those in the distant hegemon.

Another alternative to the dollar may be barter. Several bilateral development and trade deals have emerged in 2023 that sidestep the use of currencies altogether. The first was Ghana's gold-for-oil framework in February 2023. Gold is money too, of course, but commodity barter is a significant innovation with wider scope. Ghana faced a shortage of reserves and 155% inflation, but it produces gold. Gold is in high demand in oil exporting states aiming to reduce dollar assets and expropriation risks.

Economics has long taught that barter is inefficient as it relies on a 'coincidence of wants', each party must want the other's offered goods at the same time. Finding just the right party for a trade when you need something requires market discovery that few markets are adapted to provide. Money as a medium of exchange eliminates both problems: discretion over timing and place of purchase of needed goods. But for those in the world short of money, endowed generously with primary resources, barter is becoming a practical alternative to dollars to promote development.

Luke Gromen
@LukeGromen

Inflation in Ghana was 155% when they went to gold for oil in December. In the ensuing 5 months, Ghanaian inflation has collapsed to 65%.

Its unclear to me that what Ghana did was a failure. Perhaps Powell should try it?

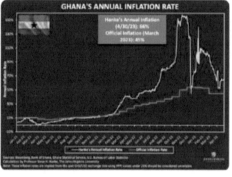

4:20 PM · May 7, 2023 · 2,623 Views

Ghana mines gold; Ghana needs oil. Many oil exporters would rather accumulate sanctions-free gold for self-custody than more sanctions-risked dollars or euros. Ghana's leaders hoped the gold for oil framework would fundamentally improve the Ghanaian balance of payments, reduce persistent depreciation of the cede, and stabilise fuel, electricity, transport, and food prices. The announcement of the oil for gold framework immediately reduced inflation, time will tell if the other objectives of this barter are achieved and sustainable. By 29 July Hanke's Inflation Roundup measured Ghana's inflation at 39%, a long way from the 8% target but trending down from triple digits.

Other barter deals are now emerging. Just after the BRICS+ Summit, newly-invited Iran announced a barter deal with China. A Chinese construction company will build a new airport in Tehran in exchange for Iranian oil shipments. China will always need oil, so there is very little risk in this deal. Iran has trouble selling oil because of Western sanctions but can ship oil to China in settlement of airport construction. The new airport with China's cutting edge private 5G network and AI-assisted cargo logistics will enhance Iran's ambition to be a logistics hub between Russia, Asia, and Africa.

Ehsan Safarnejad
@Safarnejad_IR

⚡ Iran awards $2.7bn airport project to Chinese contractor

Iran will pay for the project in crude oil.

Iran & China are not even waiting for BRICS payment system to kick in. They've already started expanding ties!

12:12 AM · Aug 28, 2023 · **165.6K** Views

Another interesting barter deal just announced is between Iran and its neighbour Iraq. Iraq has not been truly sovereign since the US brutally bombed, invaded, and occupied Iraq in 2003 after Saddam sold oil for euros. Iraq remains occupied by US bases today. An officer of the New York Fed was flown to the Green Zone shortly after occupation to set up dollar for oil export payments for Iraq. Western oil companies were keen to get contracts on Iraqi oil fields. He was a former colleague at the New York Fed, and I worked with him to get the Iraqi banking network back up to stabilise Iraq and reopen banks.[1]

Under conditions imposed by the US occupation authority, Iraq must sell oil only in dollars and the proceeds must go only to an account at the New York Fed. The US uses this

---

[1] The Iraqi Payment Network was the first national payment system to use data over satellite (the US blew up all telephone exchanges with missiles during the 'Shock and Awe' offensive). It used the newly launched Inmarsat R-BGAN satellite broadband capability. The national payment network went live for the Central Bank of Iraq and 81 bank branches nationwide in just 10 weeks, on time and on budget. I had no contract, and did not get paid, but innovated the solution and delivered the suppliers and network because I was outraged at the US and UK elective war based on fabricated 'intelligence'. I wanted to help stabilise Iraq. Andrew Bailey, now governor of the Bank of England, informally asked me for a solution to enable the planned new dinar currency exchange which commenced in October 2003.

account like a choke-chain on Iraq, freezing the account and so Iraqi fiscal capacity and import capacity, whenever Iraq does something that Washington dislikes – for over 20 years now. Iraq, formerly the most prosperous, secular, and gender-equal nation in the region remains unstable and underdeveloped after two decades of US occupation and fiscal blackmail. The New York account was frozen yet again in 2022 for Iraqi trade with Iran.

Barter frameworks may finally provide a way for the poorest nations, or those excluded by sanctions or US controls, to break out of poverty and develop their capacity. While it may be more efficient for rich nations to trade debt and dollars, poor nations may find better optionality in barter, trading what they have for what they need.

Sasha Breger Bush ✅
@IPEwithSBB

"A senior Iranian businessman says a recent deal between Iran and Iraq to swap Iranian gas and electricity for Iraqi crude oil and mazut will benefit Iran and will remove hurdles created by the US in energy trade between them." #Iraq #Iran

en.mehrnews.com
Iran to benefit from gas-for-oil barter deal with Iraq
TEHRAN, Jul. 30 (MNA) – A senior Iranian businessman says a recent deal between Iran and Iraq to swap Iranian gas and electricity for Iraqi crude oil an...

3:49 AM · Aug 29, 2023 · **891** Views

Iran may widen its non-dollar cooperation more widely. It is rebuilding a refinery for Venezuela long disabled by US sanctions. Iran also offered to build six refineries in South Africa after receiving its invitation to join BRICS+ in 2024.

 **Iran Observer** ✓
@IranObserver0   ...

Iran is currently overhauling the Paraguana refinery in Venezuela

The Paraguana refinery is Venezuela's largest oil refinery complex. It has a capacity of 955,000 barrels per day, but it has been operating at a fraction of its capacity due to US sanctions.

The overhaul is expected to restore the refinery's capacity to 700,000 barrels per day.

The completion of the overhaul is seen as a major step in Venezuela's efforts to revive its oil industry. The country's oil production has been declining in recent years, and the refinery overhaul is seen as a way to boost production and generate revenue.

7:41 PM · Aug 28, 2023 · **12.7K** Views

66 Reposts   **6** Quotes   **269** Likes   **12** Bookmarks

3 STABLE TRANSITION

According to the World Trade Organization's *Global Trade Outlook and Statistics* for 2022, merchandise trade was $25.3 trillion, services trade $6.8 trillion, digital services $3.82 trillion, and oil and gas are about $6 trillion. If total global trade is about $46 trillion altogether (with commodity, energy, and food exports included), the total value remains quite modest compared to financial flows in bonds, equities, foreign exchange, and derivatives margin. This implies that a shift to Local Currency Trade need not be destabilising or a threat to financial markets in the West.

- Bonds are over $307 trillion outstanding with international debt markets volume traded about $1.25 trillion daily in Q2 2023 (chart below), so about $315 trillion bond settlements annually.

- Repos and Triparty repos for interbank secured finance are multiples of bond trades, with Triparty Repo now totalling about $18 trillion in daily outstanding transactions and bilateral uncleared repo unknown but larger. Annual volumes probably exceed $4,000 trillion annually.

- Equities have over $108 trillion market capitalisation, with average annual market turnover about 36%, so $39 trillion annually;

- Derivatives have about $635 trillion notional value outstanding with margin held at end-2022 reported by the International Swaps and Derivatives Association (ISDA) as $1.4 trillion.

- Foreign exchange settlements average $7.5 trillion per day, peak day over $14 trillion, so a global annual turnover of about $1,900 trillion.

Rounding up, as global debt levels continue to rise into Q3 2023, about $6,000 trillion in payment flows are made in international financial settlements each year. $46 trillion, the total of all trade in goods, is less than 0.8% of those financialised payment flows. $23 trillion, the dollar share of global trade, is just 0.4%. The shift of half the dollar share to alternative currencies is just 0.2%! A gradual transition to LCT is not a systemic challenge to the dollar share of financialised world markets.

The dollar and euro will continue to be dominant in financial markets if only because the US and EU are the largest issuers of global debt securities, and these bonds dominate securities collateral as well as interest rate and currency derivatives margin flows. Being liquid markets, dollar and euro are still preferred for foreign issuance of debt as well. Even if all the dollar's share of global trade shifted to other currencies, which is unlikely as the US remains a major trade partner to many states, any impact on the financialised global economy will be marginal.

International Debt Capital Markets Volume:

This chart shows the number of deals and the volume in USD millions for the international debt capital markets from the 1st quarter of 2018 up to and including the 2nd quarter of 2023.

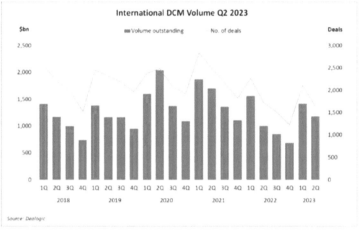

Source: Dealogic

Yen and Sterling remain relevant too, if only because their debt service is rising more rapidly. Debt interest on UK debt is now 10.4% of total government spending due to a higher proportion of inflation-linked debt.

Top 15 International DCM Volume by Currency:

This chart shows the international debt capital markets volume by currency at the end of the 2nd quarter of 2023.

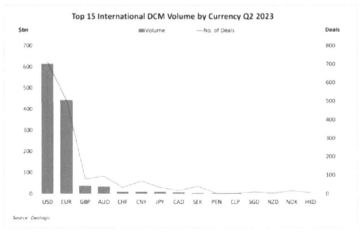

Source: Dealogic

A stable transition to LCT is best for everyone. If we all calm down, focus on getting business done, we can leave choice of currencies to those negotiating the contracts.

Whether and how quickly the world shifts from dollars to LCT alternatives is unknowable without central data collection, but the trend is evident. Quite likely use of the dollar in global trade has peaked, as suggested in Swift data. Over the two years to July 2023, dollar lost about 4% in Swift trade use while euro and yen remained stable. Chinese yuan, Indian rupee, Thai bhat, South African rand, UAE dirham, Vietnamese dong all gained substantially. Transition may accelerate but scale will remain modest and manageable in proportion to all global payments.

US sanctions policy will influence the rate of LCT adoption. Experimental data from a survey of 1,000 multinational firms in Vietnam found that as they learned of US growing use of commercial sanctions, managers' interest in cross-border payments in euro or yuan increased.[2] The broad salvos of US commercial sanctions on chips, chip fabricators, and advanced technologies will make many wary of dollar in export payment channels or use of sanctioned technologies in supply chains. Instability, war, and civil war would spur even faster LCT transition, forcing more state and non-state actors to move away from the dollar.

---

[2] McDowell, Daniel, Chapter 6: *Payment Politics: Anti-Dollar Responses to Sanctions in Trade Settlement,* Bucking the Buck: US Financial Sanctions and the International Backlash against the Dollar (March 2023). https://doi.org/10.1093/oso/9780197679876.003.0007

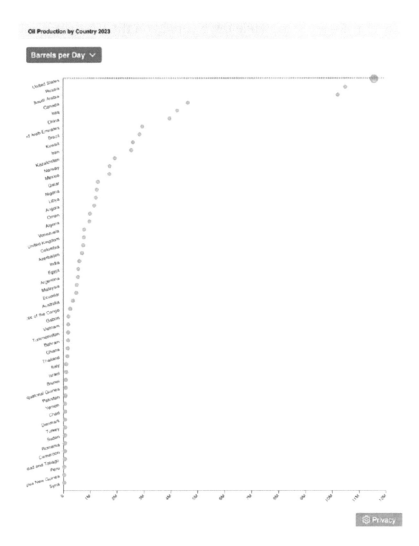

Even the Petrodollar isn't that important anymore with US being the world's top producer of oil and its federal debt risen from $475 billion in 1974 to $33 trillion in 2023. Fiscal dominance is now much more important than oil revenues to the future stability of the dollar. Interest payments on US debt are projected as the largest line item in spending in 2024. The crude oil export market is just

$2.1 trillion a year, while interest paid on the US debt is expected to exceed $3 trillion in 2024.

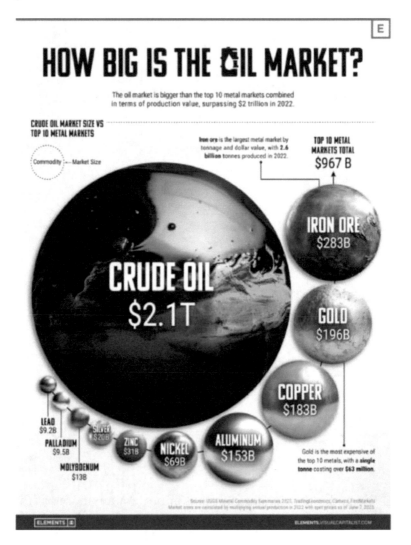

More evidence for a stable transition comes from the dollar itself. Oil traded has traded in several currencies since March 2022, and yet the dollar is not observably weakened or more volatile.

Even if OPEC states continue to diminish official reserves of USTs, relative to the size of $33 trillion debt outstanding and daily trading flows, any impact will be minimal. As of July 2023, US Treasury TIC data on foreign holdings showed Saudi Arabia held $109.2 billion (0.33%), UAE held $64.9 billion (0.2%), Kuwait $42.5 (0.13%), and Iraq $33.0 (0.1%). Rounding these four OPEC states up to $250 billion, their holdings are just 0.75% of the $33 trillion Treasuries outstanding.

The trend in Treasuries holdings is not uniform. In the year-on-year TIC data to June 2023 Saudi Arabia's holdings were down $12.4 billion, United Arab Emirates holdings were up $23.3 billion, Kuwait holdings were down $7 billion, and Iraq holdings were down $2 billion. Much of the reduced value is accounted for by valuation changes rather than investment preference. There is no indication of coordinated policy to reduce holdings. None of the OPEC states are likely to 'dump' their Treasuries unless they apprehend seizure or expropriation.

It is sanctions, aggression, and military adventures that speed declines in both global trade in dollars and foreign exchange reserves. The US might invite more confidence in dollar, Treasuries, and other US investments if it resumed realpolitik diplomacy, curbed unilateral sanctions, and complied with the UN Charter on intervention in domestic affairs of foreign states and military interventions.

It appears Russia and China will act together defend the global South from military interventions and terrorism in future. In February 2022, just before the opening of the Beijing Olympics, Russia and China issued a *Joint Statement of the Russian Federation and the People's Republic of China on the International Relations Entering a New Era and the Global*

Sustainable Development. The Statement widened bilateral cooperation:

- 'No limits' friendship between the two states;
- Shared engagement on multilateral institutions, the international economic order, Artic development, the UN 2030 Sustainable Development Goals, and bilateral economic priorities.

President Xi's three-day state visit to Russia shortly after ended with a warm farewell to President Putin: "The world is witnessing change unseen for a century, and China and Russia are the key actors driving this change."

Valerie Hopkins ✔ @VALERI... · 6 u
"Right now there are changes, the likes of which we haven't seen for 100 years," Mr. Xi told Mr. Putin through an interpreter after the state dinner as the leaders bid farewell. "And we are the ones driving these changes together."

Toon deze collectie

Already in 2023 Chinese diplomatic efforts have delivered a stunning series of peace initiatives:

- Reconciliation and restoration of embassies between Saudi Arabia and Iran;
- A peace framework for Ukraine negotiations welcomed by Russian and Ukrainian leaders;
- Efforts to gain ceasefires and negotiations for Myanmar, Yemen, and Syria;
- Peace framework for Israel and Palestine toward Palestinian sovereignty, security, and development;
- Progress resolving longstanding disputed borders with neighbour India.

Russia and China have become trusted partners to the global South because neither has an imperial past in other regions. The West's legacy of colonialism and impunity for wars in Afghanistan, Iraq, and Libya casts a very long shadow. Among all 54 African states, Ethiopia was alone in retaining its independence from European colonial rule, as a result African states regard China as a more reliable partner.

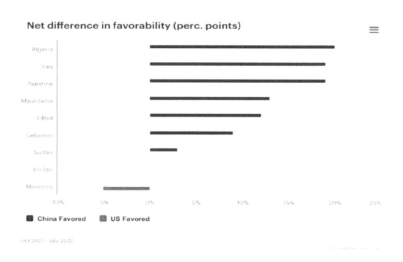

Net difference in favorability (perc. points)

Russia and China are cooperating on global South security, and BRICS+ are sharing collaborative methods of bilateral cooperation and LCT trade. Both can improve stability and resiliency. A more optimistic and collaborative world is emerging. While entrenched views in the West are slow to change, most of the world is quite happy to have sovereignty and optionality in how they trade and who they trade with.

The best strategy for the West is to let it happen, peacefully, without military aggression, clandestine destabilisations, or economic sanctions. This is the policy advocated by Kishore Mahbubani, former secretary of the UN Security Council. He favours a realpolitik pragmatism over values-based confrontations.

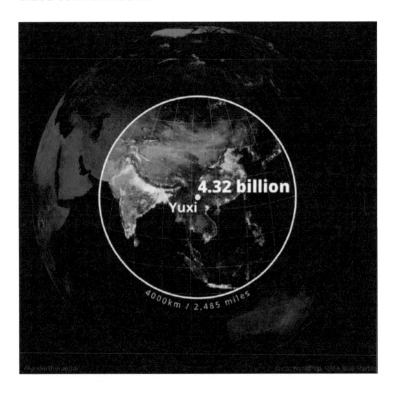

It is not just the global East and South that think a global shift from dollar is overdue. In his final 2019 Jackson Hole speech, Governor Mark Carney of the Bank of England warned of a 'destabilising asymmetry' as the US share of the global economy declines while the use of the US dollar as a global currency increases. He favoured some new synthetic basket currency on blockchain, but LCT addresses his concerns better and faster.

The West continues to dominate global wealth. Let the rest shift to LCT trade and perhaps that distribution becomes more equitable. The transition will not destabilise the West unless the fading hegemon insists on more war.

The Wealthy West

Inequality is not just limited to North versus South

longitudinal
distribution of
WEALTH

longitudinal
distribution of
POPULATION

Source: Credit Suisse Global Wealth Report 2019, Socioeconomic Data
and Applications Center - Gridded Population of the World v.11

A #MakeoverMonday Visualization
by Koen Van den Eeckhout (@koen_vde)

4 NO NEW HEGEMON

Professor Michael Hudson:
"So, the question is, how do China, Russia, Iran, and other countries break free of dollarization? Of this circular flow that is self-financing American military spending by forcing the costs onto dollar holders. Well, the answer obviously is not to use the dollar."

Historically, going back to the ancient Sea People that colonised the Mediterranean, Western empires follow a predictable pattern:

- A prosperous or resource rich rival is defeated in battle;
- Defeated elites and warriors are co-opted to serve the empire (often reinforced with elite child hostages sent to the distant empire for education, extravagant imperial privilege, and elite intermarriage);
- Common people labour in saltworks, mines, industries, and farms in the hinterland to produce tradeable wealth to pay overlords, urban elites, warriors, and tribute to the empire;

- The empire protects its colony against attack by
  rival empires, but attacks the colony in case of
  failure to pay tribute or elite or commoner rebellion;
- A port and a metropolis are ceded as sovereign to
  the empire, garrisoned with imperial warriors, and
  these colonies attract skilled and mercantile imperial
  colonists for metallurgy, salting, and mercantile
  trade throughout the empire;
- Commoners in the hinterland are kept food
  dependent, underdeveloped, uneducated,
  subordinate, unarmed, denied the benefits of
  technology, heavily taxed, and vulnerable to
  military suppression of any uprising.

Hieroglyphic record of the Sea Peoples' attack on Egypt

Since the first Baltic sea armies with bronze weapons and
ship tackle emerged from the Black Sea into the
Mediterranean, this model of Western imperialism has
served to enrich the mighty and immiserate the weak.
Metallurgy, minting of money, and fabrication of weapons
and ship tackle were exclusive to imperial ports.
Technologies were only taught to loyal imperialists. State

monopolies on money and salt ensured wealth remained concentrated, food was controlled, and goods were brought forward for taxation and tribute.

All the great mercantile capitals of the world were founded as defensible colonial outposts of empire: London, Amsterdam, New York, Buenos Aires, Hong Kong, Singapore, Tripoli, Cape Town. Some of them, like London and Tripoli, were outposts of serial empires for millennia.

Modern empire is essentially a mafia-style 'protection racket', as memorably described by US Army General Smedley Butler. To phrase it colloquially in the style of mafioso, "Nice little country you've got here. Shame should something bad happen to it. For a slice of your wealth, resources, and labour, you get to stay in charge, get very rich, and get our protection. Or else . . ."

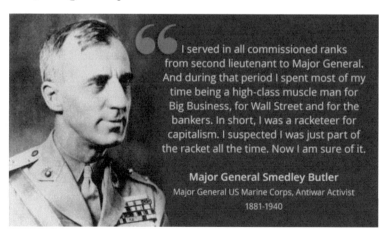

" I served in all commissioned ranks from second lieutenant to Major General. And during that period I spent most of my time being a high-class muscle man for Big Business, for Wall Street and for the bankers. In short, I was a racketeer for capitalism. I suspected I was just part of the racket all the time. Now I am sure of it.

Major General Smedley Butler
Major General US Marine Corps, Antiwar Activist
1881-1940

Bretton Woods adapted the Western imperial model to serve the interests of the United States. Negotiated with allies during wartime as they were desperate for US funding, food, weapons, trucks, tanks, planes, ammunition, and materiel. The negotiations were practically indistinguishable from blackmail. The 1944 Bretton Woods Treaty rendered signatories deeply indebted and tied long-term to their new hegemon for security. Lend-Lease obligations would endure as a drain on public treasuries into the 21st century. After the war the patents of Germany and the United Kingdom were transferred to the US for the costs of rebuilding, securing yet more long-term exploitation.

Bretton Woods founded global institutions – the United

Nations, International Monetary Fund, and World Bank – all perpetuate US global dominance with the appearance of wider international engagement and influence.

Despite the appearance of global engagement, the system still followed the ancient principles of offering protection for imperial tribute, engagement of elites in domestic exploitation, a hegemonic currency for finance, and naval patrol of global sea lanes for control of mercantile commerce. There have been few years of peace since

World War II. The US enjoys impunity as a member of the UN Security Council no matter how many wars.

US INTERVENTIONS SINCE WWII
BOMB ATTACKS, SABOTAGE, ATTEMPTED REGIME CHANGE

CHINA, 1945-46	PERU, 1965	IRAQ, 1992-1996
SYRIA, 1949	GREECE, 1967	BOSNIA, 1995
KOREA, 1950-53	GUATEMALA, 1967-69	IRAQ, 1998
CHINA, 1950-53	CAMBODIA, 1969-70	SUDAN, 1998
IRAN, 1953	CHILE, 1970-73	AFGHANISTAN, 1998
GUATEMALA, 1954	ARGENTINA, 1976	YUGOSLAVIA, 1999
TIBET, 1955-70s	ANGOLA, 1976-92	AFGHANISTAN, 2001
INDONESIA, 1958	TURKEY, 1980	IRAQ, 2002-03
CUBA, 1959	POLAND, 1980-81	SOMALIA, 2006-07
DEMOCRATIC	EL SALVADOR, 1981-92	IRAN, 2005-PRESENT
REPUBLIC OF	NICARAGUA, 1981-90	LIBYA, 2011
CONGO, 1960-65	CAMBODIA, 1980-95	VENEZUELA, 2019
DOMINICAN	LEBANON, 1982-84	YEMEN, 2013-2018
REPUBLIC, 1961	GRENADA, 1983-84	SYRIA, 2019
VIETNAM, 1961-73	LIBYA, 1986	BOLIVIA 2019
BRAZIL, 1964	IRAN, 1987-88	IRAQ, 2020
REPUBLIC OF	LIBYA, 1989	SOMALIA, 2020
CONGO, 1964	PHILIPPINES, 1989	AFGHANISTAN, 2020
GUATEMALA, 1964	PANAMA, 1989-90	SYRIA, 2021
LAOS, 1964-73	IRAQ, 1991	
DOMINICAN	KUWAIT, 1991	
REPUBLIC, 1965-66	SOMALIA, 1992-94	redfish

Debt was feature of US hegemony. Weak states were encouraged to borrow 'for development' from the World Bank or IMF, but the money too often went to corrupt elites or back to Western corporations through investment subsidies. Elites and their children enjoyed extravagant lifestyles, while their states remained exploited, uneducated, lacking infrastructure, and poor. Elites' children went to top Western universities and got jobs in Western banks, think tanks, and journalism. Like the hostages offered by elites to ancient Athens or Rome, these empire-educated young provided both a bridge and implied leverage against any rebellion or reform.

States were required by conditionality on IMF and World Bank loans to 'open' their economies to foreign investment. Western corporations bought up productive lands and resources such as plantations, oil fields, and mines. A few trading companies intermediated supply to refineries and processors at huge profits, cementing tight control globally over most food, energy, and commodities trade. Profits and wealth accumulated in the West. The poor of the East and South laboured for poverty wages under conditions of huge inequality and vulnerability.

Crops grown in the developing world were for export, not local consumption: rubber, cocoa, coffee, palm oil. Local food production was suppressed to make poor countries import dependent, permanently at risk of food poverty if they revolted. Even states blessed with abundant arable land were discouraged from self-sufficiency.

Most of the world embraces food as a human right. A recent UN vote recognising food as a human right had just two 'opposed' votes: US and Israel. As states shift to Local Currency Trade many are actively exploring food security and agricultural reforms as a national security policy.

US hegemony first began to be questioned as the US ran ever larger trade and fiscal deficits during the Vietnam War. Large trade partners in Europe began to exchange dollars for gold at the Bretton Woods Treaty rate of $35 per ounce. The US had gained the largest gold reserves in the world from financing combatants in World War I and World War II and reconstruction of Europe post-war. As gold shipped eastwards, the US threatened redeemers as of old with denial of 'protection'.

Deutsche Bundesbank
Historisches Archiv
Wilhelm-Epstein-Str. 14
60431 Frankfurt am Main

By refraining from dollar conversions into gold from the United States Treasury the Bundesbank has intended to contribute to international monetary cooperation and to avoid any disturbing effects on the foreign exchange and gold markets. You may be assured that also in the future the Bundesbank intends to continue this policy and to play its full part in contributing to international monetary cooperation.

Sincerely yours,

Karl Blessing

The Blessing Letter, above, was written in 1967 during the Cold War. By 1967 many countries in Europe were worried about growing US trade and fiscal deficits. They redeemed dollars for gold and spurned buying US Treasuries with their dollars. Gold purchases as official reserves hit a record in 1967 not matched again until 2022.

Bundesbank President Karl Blessing was pressured to commit in writing that Germany would not redeem dollars, enabling ever larger US deficits. Blessing himself explained the context of the Letter in a 1971 *Der Spiegel* interview. By then France and Britain were demanding more gold for dollars too.

QUESTION: You mean the threat of the Americans: If you don't support the dollar in this way, will we withdraw the troops from the Federal Republic?

BLESSING: It was never an outspoken threat, but the threat was always there in the background. Former High Commissioner McCloy was in the German government once and said: Look, we've had a Senate decision now; there will soon be a majority that we withdraw our boys. We have to do something. So he called me at home at three thirty on a Sunday afternoon and said, "I have to fly back tonight, can't we see each other?" And I said to him, "My dear McCloy, your situation is clear, that's a You have a balance of payments problem, nothing more. You have seen that we are sensible and do not convert our dollars into gold. I'm willing to even give you that in writing for a period of time. Unfortunately, the letter I wrote back then is still valid today. **5**

Many resource rich states were targeted for political destabilisation or coups to preserve US influence, corporate and financial exploitation, and extend dollar dominance. This list is too long and the world wearies of the hegemonic threat.

Brazil makes an interesting example because past president Dilma Rousseff is now president of the New Development Bank in Shanghai ('BRICS bank'). As a leader of a reform movement in her youth, Rousseff was harassed, arrested, tortured, and imprisoned by a brutal regime installed by the US to promote corporate exploitation. Even as president, she was not secure. The US tapped her phones and email, created a scandal with selective leaking to aligned media and rivals, and had her removed in a soft coup. Her US-backed successor Bolsonaro dedicated his impeachment vote to Rousseff's torturer.

Nowhere was the protection racket clearer than the Petrodollar. In 1974 US Treasury Secretary William Simon and Secretary of State Henry Kissinger made a secret flight to Saudi Arabia. Negotiating like mobsters with King Faisal, they threatened the extermination of the King and his family followed by US military occupation of Saudi oil fields, unless King Faisal agreed to sell Saudi oil only for dollars and secretly purchased US Treasuries with the proceeds. He agreed, and that deal was respected by his heirs. Similar deals were struck with the Shah of Iran and other dependent rulers willing to accede to US 'protection'. Any that resisted were replaced with US-chosen dictators from cadres of US-trained military officers such as Saddam in Iraq and Gaddafi in Libya.

In the 21st century the Petrodollar hegemonic violence continued and intensified: Iraq, Libya, Syria, Yemen, Venezuela. All had leaders seeking to sell oil for other currencies than dollar. All were destroyed militarily and/or immiserated by sanctions. US military occupation of both Iraq and Syria persists today.

Key Findings

- 432,093 civilians have died violent deaths as a direct result of the U.S. post-9/11 wars.

- An estimated 3.6-3.8 million people have died indirectly in post-9/11 war zones, bringing the total death toll to at least 4.5-4.7 million and counting.

- More than 7.6 million children under five in post-9/11 war zones are suffering from acute malnutrition

- War deaths from malnutrition and a damaged health system and environment likely far outnumber deaths from combat.

Source: Watson Institute for International and Public Affairs, August 2023

Libya is particularly tragic. France was concerned it was

losing its valuable Libyan oil concessions. The US feared Gaddafi would establish a pan-African currency backed by gold. The most prosperous African nation, with free education, free healthcare, free housing, free food, was reduced by NATO airstrikes, rival warlords, and terrorism to extreme poverty with open air slave markets. Worse, the destruction of Libya destabilised all of north Africa, leading to mass migrations through Libya to Europe. Europe itself is now destabilised, with right wing anti-immigration parties gaining power. Gadaffi had warned of this before his death, but NATO did not heed his warning.

Now listen you, people of NATO. You're bombing a wall which stood in the way of African migration to Europe, and in the way of Al-Qaeda terrorists. This wall was Libya. You're breaking it. You're idiots, and you will burn in Hell for thousands of migrants from Africa and for supporting Al-Qaeda. It will be so.|

Source: Wikileaks

No one knows how many more countries will be destroyed in maintaining US hegemony. The US is intensifying illegal base construction in Syria, has deployed more ships and troops to the Persian Gulf in summer 2023, and also builds new missile bases on Pacific islands nearest China in Japan, the Philippines, and Guam. All activity indicates the US is preparing more wars to conserve its hegemony.

Glenn Diesen @ @Glenn_Diesen · 20h
General Mark Milley, the chairman of the US Joint Chiefs of Staff, told Jordanian TV on Thursday that US forces illegally occupying oil fields in Syria's northeast will remain there for "many, many years" to come

zerohedge.com
US Military Likely To Remain In Syria For "Many, Many Years" To Come: Milley

○ 147   ↻ 719   ♡ 1,017   ili 105K   ⤴

War in Asia would be particularly disruptive to the global economy. More than half of all humans on Earth live in Southeast Asia. The Yuxi Circle is a geographic projection of this huge concentration of humanity. War in the region will bring unspeakable chaos and harm. Preparation for war by half of humanity will also spur inflation in energy and food as they must stockpile against the looming threat of supply disruptions.

Even allies are at risk. Japan and Taiwan are particularly dependent on imported energy and food. The scale of human tragedy should war come to the region is immense.

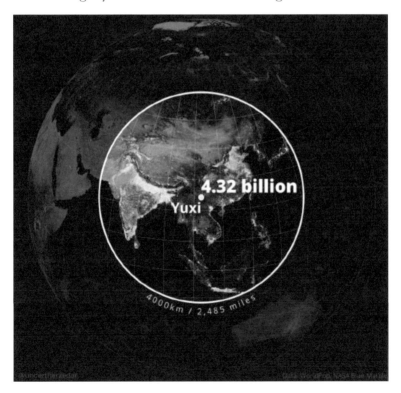

Even as oil prices rise, US-led militarisation accelerates. The US now has more than 200 military bases, 385,000 troops, scattered around the South China Sea. China has responded to the militarisation by building just two new airstrips on island bases. Defending its homeland, China strengthens threat detection, air defences, and sea patrols. The Pentagon's own war gaming foretells catastrophic losses of ships and men in the first hours of any war, but this does not curb the plans for war or the building of new bases.

In December 2022 Japan changed from a defensive

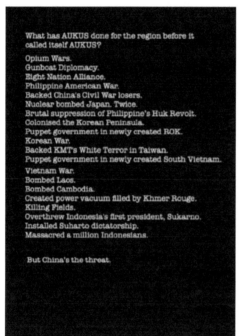

What has AUKUS done for the region before it called itself AUKUS?

Opium Wars.
Gunboat Diplomacy.
Eight Nation Alliance.
Philippine American War.
Backed China's Civil War losers.
Nuclear bombed Japan. Twice.
Brutal suppression of Philippine's Huk Revolt.
Colonised the Korean Peninsula.
Puppet government in newly created ROK.
Korean War.
Backed KMT's White Terror in Taiwan.
Puppet government in newly created South Vietnam.
Vietnam War.
Bombed Laos.
Bombed Cambodia.
Created power vacuum filled by Khmer Rouge.
Killing Fields.
Overthrew Indonesia's first president, Sukarno.
Installed Suharto dictatorship.
Massacred a million Indonesians.

But China's the threat.

military policy held since 1945 to embrace the prospect of offensive first strikes. Japan agreed to buy 400 Tomahawk missiles from the US for placement on new island missile bases nearest China's coast. The missiles will be paid for by Japan but under US military command. They can be used for a first strike on China without Japanese military consent or foreknowledge.

The AUKUS alliance announced in September 2021 between the US, UK, and Australia appears explicitly oriented to preparing war in the Pacific. Australia hosts US nuclear-capable bombers and three Virginia Class nuclear submarines.

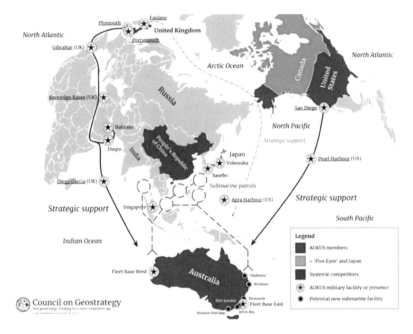

Australia will also purchase 220 Tomahawk Land Attack missiles for $1.3 billion. As with Japan, Australia will not have discretion over the nature of US weaponry deployed from its territory or its subs. Like Japan, Australia has the privilege of purchasing the subs and missiles, but the US Navy will have command of the vessels. US Navy captains will determine use of the subs in attacking or blockading China in a war.

The end of the Petrodollar will realign East Asia-West Asia trade and security. In January 2023 Saudi's Foreign Minister HH Prince Faisal bin Farhan confirmed at Davos that Saudi would sell its oil for other currencies than dollar. Although Treasury Secretary Yellen has since asked for a Saudi commitment not to sell oil for other currencies. To reinforce this request the US has deployed US Navy vessels capable of extensive airstrikes and landing operations with 3,000 additional troops to the Persian Gulf in July, supplementing the tens of thousands of US troops and hundreds of aircraft already on US bases in the region, including bases in Saudi Arabia itself.

These are uncertain times, but there is cause for optimism that the LCT transition can proceed peacefully, if only because there will be no rival hegemon in the new order.

China, which lost 35 million lives fighting imperial Japan as an ally in World War II, has not engaged in any military adventures beyond border conflicts and Vietnam since 1949. It has just one foreign naval base. In its thousands of years' history, China has traded widely in its region without military aggression or colonisation of its neighbours. President Xi said at the BRICS Business Summit in South Africa on 22 August 2023 that China will not be a new hegemon: 'Hegemonism is not in China's DNA'.

Devon Dave
@dave_odo

@JanetYellenSec predicts #Dollar decline

#BRICS #Russia #China #Saudi_Arabia #Brazil #Argentina

"US Secretary of Treasury Janet Yellen this week warned that there would be "slow decline" in the US dollar as the global reserve currency"

unherd.com
Janet Yellen: expect a slow decline in US dollar dominance
US Secretary of Treasury Janet Yellen this week warned that there would be "slow decline" in the US dollar as the global reserve currency. Asked if the US …

2:29 PM · Jun 16, 2023 · **67** Views

China stays committed to an independent foreign policy of peace and the building of a community with a shared future for mankind. As a developing country and a member of the Global South, China breathes the same breath with other developing countries and pursues a shared future with them. China has resolutely upheld the common interests of developing countries and worked to increase the representation and voice of EMDCs in global affairs. Hegemonism is not in China's DNA; nor does China have any motivation to engage in major-power competition. China stands firmly on the right side of history, and believes that a just cause should be pursued for the common good.

Russia lost 27 million lives as an ally defeating Axis powers Germany and Japan in World War II. Russia has had no foreign military adventures since 1991, when the Russian Federation emerged from the fracturing Soviet Union. In the 21st century Russia has only threatened military retaliation against those attacking Russian peoples, as in the ethnically Russian republics of Donetsk and Luhansk in Ukraine, or the territory of the Russian Federation itself. Russia is therefore an unlikely hegemon.

India, Brazil, and South Africa were all colonies rather than empires, and are unlikely to transform into imperial states for regional or global military adventures.

BRICS+ itself cannot be hegemonic. It has no leadership, no hierarchy, no permanent officers, no military, no weaponry, no rules, no headquarters, and no functional website. BRICS+ is a cooperative holacracy, where each sovereign nation chooses its own roles, purposes, domains, and accountability. Decisions are taken by consensus among peers, with issues raised and discussed in periodic governance meetings. BRICS+ has no power to punish or compel use of any currency, even if its members could agree on one. It certainly cannot project military force.

Nicole Grajewski @NicoleGrajewski · 11h
BRICS is an informal organization with no charter, no secretariat, no established criteria for membership, and no procedures on expansion - it doesn't even have a functioning website.

◯ 48　　↺ 149　　♡ 516　　ᶴⁱ 89K　　↥

BRICS+ and its aligned states in the global East and South do not need or want a hegemon to rival or replace the US. Nor is a hegemon needed for bilateral LCT with all currencies as eligible options. The hegemon compels the use of a single currency, but the direction of the world is toward free choice to elect any currency.

BRICS+ is effective at promoting bilateral cooperation among its members. For example, immediately following the invitation to Iran to join BRICS+, Iran offered to develop 5 oil refineries in South Africa. Iran had previously replaced turbines made by Siemens with turbines of its own design to relieve Russia of the burden of German and Canadian servicing of old turbines. These bilateral cooperations build rather than destroy.

Mick Wallace ✔ @wallacemick · 9h

No country in the world has invaded more countries in the last 75 years as the #US - They have shown so little respect for the Sovereignty of other Nations, so little respect for the #UN Charter, so little respect for the Human Rights of citizens in less powerful countries...

> **Department of State** ✔ @StateDept · 1d
>
> .@SecBlinken: "Governments that violate human rights are almost always the same ones that flout other key parts of that order – such as invading, coercing, and threatening other countries, or breaking trade rules." The U.S. will continue to take a stand for human rights for all.

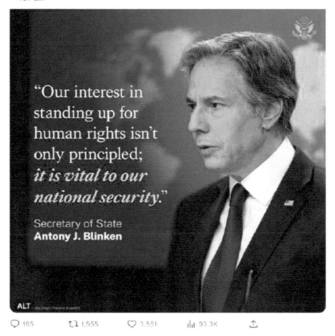

"Our interest in standing up for human rights isn't only principled; *it is vital to our national security.*"

Secretary of State
Antony J. Blinken

ALT

💬 165   🔁 1,555   ♡ 3,551   📊 93.3K   ⬆

If the US accepts LCT transition gracefully, it could improve living conditions for Americans at home. Despite its massive wealth as a nation, infrastructure, education, healthcare, crime, drug addiction, infant mortality, and youth mortality are all worse in US than in peer states. Better is possible for Americans at home if spending on foreign bases, wars, and clandestine operations abroad to conserve hegemony is diverted to improving life at home.

Life expectancy vs. health expenditure

Our World in Data

From 1970 to 2018

Data source: OECD — Note: Health spending measures the consumption of health care goods and services, including personal health care (curative care, rehabilitative care, long-term care, ancillary services, and medical goods) and collective services (prevention and public health services as well as health administration), but excluding spending on investments.
Shown is total health expenditure (financed by public and private sources).   Licensed under CC-BY by the author Max Roser.

OurWorldInData.org — Research and data to make progress against the world's largest problems.

TOM GAULD

The optionality of Multicurrency Mercantilism ensures that if any state becomes too powerful, too aggressive, too violent against the vulnerable, then trade and finance can shift to other currencies. This is happening now with dollar, after too many elective wars and sanctions, but in future commerce could shift from any other currency if a state threatened or destabilised its peers and partners. Any currency can be embraced, and any currency can be shunned. No hegemon is needed to instil order, and collective objection to inappropriate conduct becomes collective action to curb abuse.

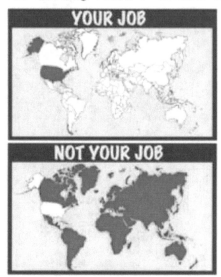

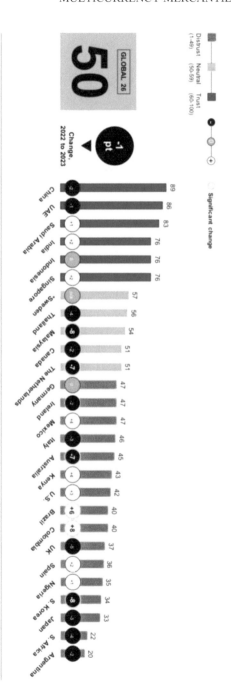

73

SECRET TWO-PART ASIAN PLAN TO
DESTROY WESTERN CIVILIZATION

STEP ONE
WAIT FOR THEM TO DESTROY THEMSELVES

STEP TWO
CURRY

ti You reposted

The Young Pretender 🦍 **#SilverSqueeze**
@Dioclet54046121

Dollars fans think that because there has been no overriding announcement, little is happening. A change of season does not need to be announced in order to happen.

4:38 PM · Aug 28, 2023 · **238** Views

5 GLOBALISATION ACCELERATES

While Western media talks about decoupling and de-risking supply chain dependence on Russia and China, data shows globalisation still accelerating at a brisk pace. China's decade of Bridge & Road Initiative (BRI) investment in ports, railways, and roads pays off with growing regional and global trade in all BRI regions. BRI trade with China is now bigger than US and EU trade combined. And all global regions grow more strongly than the sclerotic, self-sanctioned West.

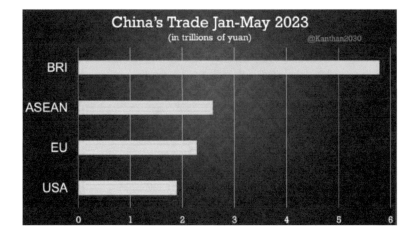

BRICS+ will drive the pace of globalisation through cooperative engagement and investments. Following the BRICS+ XV Summit, UAE Economy Minister Al Marri explained to Bloomberg that UAE will use the BRICS+ membership to cement UAE as a global mercantile and financial hub and grow trade with the global South tenfold. This is ambitious, but not impossible. Dubai has already taken over oil and gas trading from Geneva in 2023, and grows market share in gold trading as well. According to the Financial Times, 8 of the top 20 biggest traders of Russian crude are registered in Dubai while Switzerland retains just one entry. UAE has the expertise and financial capacity to drive energy and commodities exploration and investments in Africa, Latin America, and other regions.

UAE-registered companies were the biggest traders of Russian crude oil and refined products in the first four months of 2023

Top 20 buyers of Russian oil and refined products by value, Jan-Apr 2023 ($)

Crude oil ▾

Source: FT analysis of Russian customs declarations
* Some of Gunvor's trades were made by its Swiss entity. Some of Vitol's trades were by its Bahrain entity

FINANCIAL TIMES

Kathleen Tyson ✓
@Kathleen_Tyson_

I love the ambition in the UAE. Economy Minister Al Marri wants to grow UAE trade with the global South tenfold as a BRICS+ member.

> **B** **Bloomberg Middle East** ✓ **B** @middleeast · Aug 28
>
> "We are focusing on our global trade, the UAE has always been a global hub."
>
> Joining the BRICS won't come to the detriment of ties with the West, Economy Minister Abdulla bin Touq Al Marri tells @ManusCranny trib.al/bTtJUhF

> Abdulla Bin Touq
> Al Marri
> UAE ECONOMY MINISTER

> 0:34 Exclusive UAE INVITED TO JOIN BRICS

4:32 PM · Aug 28, 2023 · **5,260** Views

De-risking dependence on China has been policy rhetoric but not commercial reality. Companies closing plants in Europe as more expensive energy renders them uneconomic have built new plants in China more than anywhere else. China quite simply has the best manufacturing ecosystem, workforce, logistics, and management. Even if companies choose an alternative Asian manufacturing location, most components will be sourced from China.

No company can be a globally competitive and prosperous company if it cuts off 1.4 billion Chinese consumers from its market. Europe and the US do not offer the same scale of consumtion and their workers have not had real wage growth for decades. Chinese workers have quadrupled average wages from $2 an hour at the start of the century to more than $8 an hour now, and lead Asia in share of job entrants with university degrees.

Most global growth is in Asia, and most growing investment and trade is in Asia too. It makes sense to expand where the market is.

Agathe Demarais @AgatheDemarais · 19h

Asia's economic model is changing fast
• "Factory Asia" is increasingly producing for Asian countries, instead of shipping goods to US & Europe
• More regional trade means more capital flows across Asia, further deepening region's integration

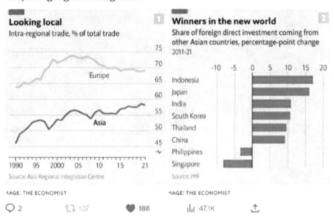

❑ 2   ↻ 107   ♥ 186   ᐧᐧᐧ 47.1K   ⬆

Agathe Demarais @AgatheDemarais · 20h   ...

■■ ■■ - Europe's de-risking plans: rhetoric vs. practice
• Despite de-risking hype, more than two-thirds of EU companies do not plan to shift away from China
• Firms that de-risk often go to ASEAN - but ASEAN countries could well be transit hub for Chinese goods

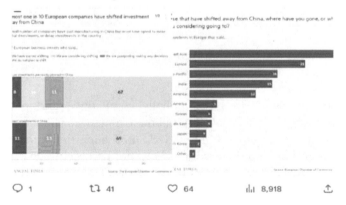

❑ 1   ↻ 41   ♡ 64   ᐧᐧᐧ 8,918   ⬆

Globalisation also accelerates because shared trade, technology, and telecommunications will drive acceleration. US companies target the G7 market almost exclusively, but Chinese companies find opportunities more widely. The largest phone company in Africa is Transsion, a Chinese company that sold its first phone in 2007, but has never sold a phone in China. Transsion makes its phones and sells its phones in Africa, where it now has a 54% market share, 11.7% of the global market.

The success of the company has some amazing elements:

- 16 of 20 mangers at the Ethiopian Transsion plant are Ethiopian and just 4 are Chinese;
- With 400 employees, most administrators and engineers are locals (Ethiopian universities graduate 70,000 each year);
- All price points are covered from $10 basic phone to $1,300 flagship smartphone;
- Acid-proof shells extend useful life of phones even in hot and humid local conditions;
- Camera algorithm is optimised for African faces and skin tones;
- Keyboards and AI voice services for all major African languages;
- Multiple SIM cards and standby capability to access different networks or call four different numbers simultaneously. (Many Africans still have multiple SIMs because network integration lags and cross-network charges are higher.)

As Chinese companies shift across borders to localise their products and build secure partnerships, globalisation must intensify. Everyone will have access to the global market.

Even de-risking to 'friendshore' supply chains makes globalisation accelerate. The US put pressure on companies to shift manufacturing out of China to other third-party countries, and that has happened to some extent. But it only means that China exports more with the countries with new plants because China remains essential to supply of components. Mexico, Canada (now top 2 US trade partners), Vietnam, Korea, and Japan have absorbed the Chinese exports that used to go to the US. They re-export after finishing production, but US pays higher costs.

The other driver of more rapid globalisation is the full integration of countries hit by US sanctions. Currency optionality reintegrates these states in the global economy. 30 countries, 28% of global population, are subject to more than 26,000 sanctions by the US, EU, UK, Canada, and others. 22,000 of the sanctions have been applied since 2000. As trading networks shift to LCT, these 30 states will grow and prosper.

Un problema global

Un total **26.162** sanciones aplicadas a **30 naciones.**

A **9 países** le han sido impuestas **25.152** sanciones, **96%** de estas medidas.

Mientras que **4%** (1010 medidas) están distribuidas en los **21** países restantes.

www.observatorio.gob.ve

MCU impuestas en el mundo
Actualizado a agosto 2023

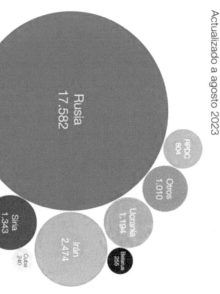

Rusia
17.582

RPDC
804

Otros
1.010

Irak
330

Venezuela
970

Ucrania
1.194

Siria
1.343

Cuba
240

Irán
2.474

Bielorrusia
265

Fuente: OFAC-EE.UU / Unión Europea /
Fuentes oficiales / www.castellum.ai

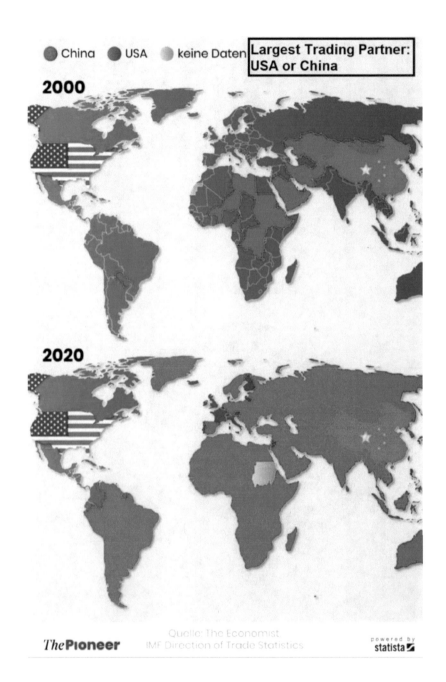

China ● USA ● keine Daten | Largest Trading Partner: USA or China

2000

2020

Quelle: The Economist,
IMF Direction of Trade Statistics

powered by
statista

6 BEWARE THE ANGELL PARADOX

It is part of the moral tragedy with which we are dealing that words like 'democracy,' 'freedom,' 'rights,' 'justice,' which have so often inspired heroism and have led men to give their lives for things which make life worthwhile, can also become a trap, the means of destroying the very things men desire to uphold.
- Sir Norman Angell

Sir Norman Angell was a brilliant journalist, monetary theorist, and peace activist. He won the 1934 Nobel Peace Prize for an insight in his 1910 book *The Great Illusion*: Economic sanctions between interdependent developed nations at war will leave both sides poorer whoever wins because sanctions undermine and devalue all similar assets, contracts, trade, and credit. His 1912 *Money Game* teaches the nature of gold-backed money and mercantilism and was a huge hit, taught in schools and played in clubs in North America and Europe. In 1932 he published *The Unseen Assassins*, warning that patriotism, nationalism, and imperialism threatened to undermine all aspects of civil society. 1938 *Peace with Dictators?* probed the challenge of collective security and limits of national sovereignty and defence.

Angell's activism for sound money, peaceful development, free trade, greater interdependence between states, advocacy for collective security, and improved education became known as *Angellism*. *The Great Illusion* sold over 2 million copies and was translated to 25 languages. But as *Monopoly* displaced *The Money Game* on school and club shelves after Bretton Woods, the principles of mercantilist trade gave way to dollar dominance, and Angell was largely forgotten.

The Angell Paradox is ever more relevant in the 21st century, as all economies are now integrated as a global economy with global interdependence. Excessive unilateral sanctions, especially the unprecedented scale of sanctions against Russia and China, have undermined global confidence in Western assets, rule of law, commercial contracts, and technology suppliers. Yet the West refuses to see the dangers of undermining the basis of its past success.

I know of Angell and his works only because I rented his house for a weekend holiday with several families and friends. We then rented it twice more as it is unique and wonderful. Angell built his home by his own industry on an island in the Blackwater Estuary near his family's farm in Essex. Most of the house is wood scavenged from shipwrecks on the island or surrounding tidal reaches. The fireplace is bits of marble rubble collected after the House of Lords was bombed in World War II. A room atop a tower offers a splendid view over the estuary.

The library holds a collection of Sir Norman's books. I have bought many of them for my own library since.

Perhaps it is the chance rental of that holiday home that prepared me for explaining what Multicurrency Mercantilism and its peace dividend can bring now.

Even before war started in Ukraine, I was warning that projected Western sanctions would harm the West as much as Russia. The warning was refused publication. Distributed privately, only the French took the warning seriously. They have managed the energy and inflation crisis that debilitates and de-industrialises much of Europe better than others.

The following was drafted 23 February 2022, on the eve of war in Ukraine:

_____

Central banks didn't need another complex challenge, but they have one with the crisis in the Donbass region between Ukraine and Russia. Donbass was integral to Russia until 1954 ceded it to Ukraine. More than 90 percent of the population is ethnically Russian. The Donetsk and Luhansk Peoples Republics self-declared independence from Ukraine in 2014 after a popular referendum. The Republics were signatories to the 2015 Minsk Agreement providing for their autonomy within Ukraine. The Agreement was never implemented, leaving their status undetermined. Meanwhile Ukraine banned Russian as a language, and refused the Donbass populations passports, public benefits, and pensions. Right-wing militias subjected the Republics to violent attacks and sabotage, leading to reprisals.

Beginning late last year Ukraine accumulated huge inflows of munitions, materiel, and troops from NATO nations in preparation for a loudly proclaimed invasion from Russia. Russia massed troops near the borders this year, creating a stand-off and flurry of diplomatic exchanges.

Over the weekend shelling from Ukrainian positions in the west destroyed civilian electricity and water supply plants in the Donbass, and large explosions hit urban capitals. Women and children were evacuated to Russia where most have family and friends to take them in. On Monday evening President Putin recognised the Republics as autonomous, as provided in the Minsk Agreement, and pledged economic and military support to defend Republic territories and populations. On Tuesday the Russian parliament authorised the deployment of Russian forces beyond Russian borders. Also on Tuesday, the EU, UK, and US announced sanctions against both the Republics and Russia.

1933 Nobel Peace Prize awarded to Angell in London's Imperial War Museum.

Sir Norman Angell won the Nobel Peace Prize in 1933, principally for his 1910 thesis *The Great Illusion*. He argued that developed, integrated economies cannot profit from war, even if victorious. Credit and contractual interconnections between developed nations mean that regardless of who wins no one gets richer. Europe and the world are far more financialised, globalised and interconnected in 2022. If Angell is still right, yesterday's EU, UK and US sanctions may undermine credit, contractual certainty, and markets, impoverishing us all.

The summary below is from the 1913 edition:

[Angell] establishes this apparent paradox, in so far as the economic problem is concerned, by showing that wealth in the economically civilized world is founded upon credit and commercial contract (these being the outgrowth of an economic interdependence due to the increasing division of labour and greatly developed communication). If credit and commercial contract are tampered with in an attempt at confiscation, the credit-dependent wealth is undermined, and its collapse involves that of the conqueror; so that if conquest is not to be self-injurious it must respect the enemy's property, in which case it becomes economically futile.

Russia is a nation with a trade surplus from exports of energy and food, the two largest factors in the current global inflationary surge. Concerns about the stability of supplies of wheat, oil, and natural gas as armaments flowed into Ukraine had already driven prices sharply higher in global markets, to Russia's advantage. Oil is now near USD 100 per barrel. The EU, UK and US have suffered a severe energy crisis and inflationary shock from higher energy and food prices, dampening recovery from the pandemic and forcing central banks toward raising interest rates.

Germany's suspension of the Nord Stream 2 pipeline approval process yesterday spurred EU natural gas and energy prices even higher. This particularly hurts EU industries that for decades relied on stable, low-cost, long-term energy contracts for Russian gas and electricity generation. Higher energy costs in EU, UK and US divert industrial finances from investment and consumer expenditure from wider consumption. That dampens growth in domestic economies and hurts fiscal revenues.

The US has risen to be the top exporter of LNG globally over the past decade, and now has seven LNG export terminals. No doubt this weighed in US opposition to the Nord Stream 2 pipeline.

Industrial and consumer demand destruction from currently high prices in importers UK and EU will place a drag on future LNG demand from the US as well as Russia and other rivals. The pivot to greener energy will be reinforced. US exports of LNG may gain from the Donbass crisis in the short-term but suffer longer-term. Rust Belt industries in the US may gain briefly from destruction of industrial rivals in the UK and EU but will still lag Asia in competitiveness. China this month secured long-term energy stability in an agreement for Russian gas valued at USD 117 billion.

German industrial companies may also lose to rivals over the Nord Stream 2 suspension. Russia has invested USD 10 billion, but much of that went to German companies working on the project. Rivals may say that Germany is now an unreliable partner for infrastructure development, costing German companies global revenues from rising infrastructure investments.

Yesterday's economic sanctions against Russia are likely to undermine the credibility and appeal of domestic financial markets too. The US banned US investors buying primary issues of Russian debt in 2014 and US banks from participation in non-rouble sovereign bonds from 2019. Yesterday the US announced it will ban trading of Russian sovereign debt in US secondary markets from March 1. Both issuers and investors in sovereign debt may now view US markets with suspicion. The immediate impact of the proposed trading ban yesterday was to crash prices of Russian sovereign debt, hurting portfolio investors, not Russia.

The UK cannot ban Russian sovereign debt without legislation, so announcing a ban on primary issues. Putting London's secondary markets at hazard appears unusually lawless. London's strength as an international trade and capital market has been 1000 years of non-discriminatory rule of law. The Johnson government should be wary of signalling to the world that this mercantile principle that has served London so well has now weakened.

The EU, UK and US may need Russian finance more than Russia needs their markets. Russia has exercised consistent fiscal discipline over the past decade, where the US, UK and EU have indulged in budgetary excesses. Sovereign debt in the US and euro area now exceeds 100 percent of GDP; UK debt is now 94 percent of GDP. Russia does not need foreign finance, but it makes choices about where to invest, and yesterday's sanctions will weigh in those choices.

Russia has the world's 4th largest official reserves, USD 634 billion in January 2022, with the largest proportion held in gold, then EUR, then USD. Gold is rising on war and inflation jitters. Russia's official reserves asset management strategy pays off two ways. The National Wealth Fund, which contributes to Russian public pensions, also holds more than USD 600 billion in gold and foreign currency reserves.

Both the Central Bank of the Russian Federation and the National Wealth Fund had already determined to reduce holdings of USD and GBP assets in the wake of the 2014 sanctions. Many other central banks and sovereign wealth funds are now watching. Concerns about the politicisation of USD and GBP-denominated reserves have risen after expropriation of Central Bank of Venezuela USD assets by US authorities in 2019, expropriation of Central Bank of Venezuela GBP assets and gold by UK authorities in 2020, and expropriation of Central Bank of Afghanistan USD assets in 2022. Peer custody of official reserves in the Federal Reserve Bank of New York and Bank of England is not 'riskless' if a claim can be expropriated by unilateral decree to destabilise the nation of a depositing central bank.

Sanctions against Russian banks and individuals announced yesterday may prove similarly counter-productive to global confidence in the longer term. There is no suggestion or evidence of law-breaking by the banks and persons sanctioned, nor any suggestion that the banks and individuals contributed to events in the Donbass or the Russian determination to recognise and defend the Republics. The banks and individuals are sanctioned merely because they are Russian, they own assets abroad, and they are said to have powerful friends in the Russian government. Moreover, there is no due process offered where sanctions can be weighed at law before these freezes or expropriations become effective. There is no clear right of appeal at law. A reputation for capriciously freezing or seizing assets from random rich foreigners creates a perception of lawlessness that discourages investment. This is particularly dangerous in 2022 as concentration of private wealth inequality has seen more than USD 14 trillion accumulate in so-called 'family offices' globally.

What was true of interconnected economies and war in 1910 may be more true of our globalised economy in 2022. When developed nations connected by credit and contract come into conflict, even those who deem themselves victorious may not profit. We may all pay the price of yesterday's sanctions against Russia for a long time to come in global energy and food inflation and insecurity, higher interest rates, loss of industrial capacity and domestic consumption, loss of investment appeal in our sovereign debt and capital markets, and loss of reputation for abiding by due process and a non-discriminatory rule of law.

For something written in a rush under conditions of uncertainty, the commentary holds up well. The West has alienated its global creditors. Central banks are buying record gold and spurning sovereign bonds. The US is seeking to strip Europe of industry by subsidising relocation of plants into the US with the Inflation Reduction Act.

The global East and South that once favoured passive Western investment now seek active investments in each other through joint enterprise and co-development.

Whatever 'rule of law' advantage the West held has been badly eroded by asset freezes, expropriations, and technology sanctions – all without due process or right of appeal.

≡ **BARRON'S**

Subscribe Today. Sign In

"[I]f Western economies no longer treat property rights as sacrosanct, why should capital keep flowing from the 'greater South' into the 'unified West'?" writes Louis-Vincent Gave, CEO of research firm Gavekal.

Maybe it won't. In January, foreign investors sold $36.6 billion of U.S. Treasuries, according to Citigroup data, the fourth month of outflows over the past five. And while the actual dollar amount has risen 6.8% since the end of 2019, the percentage of U.S. government debt held by foreigners has fallen to 29.3%, from 39.2% at the end of 2019.

More than that, Western sanctions are demonstrably ineffective for the stated aims. They have failed to weaken the states they target sufficiently for the political changes sought. Cuba, Iran, Afghanistan, Venezuela, Syria, and now Russia and China remain defiant in the face of sanctions.

Russia has prospered from Western sanctions, becoming a trusted partner in the global South for energy, fertiliser, and food. Russian cooperation is sought for security against neo-imperialists and terrorism. Evident success on the battlefield, scaling military production, and rapid military technology advances, proven electronic warfare, superior missile defences, and drones will lead more states to seek Russian military cooperation.

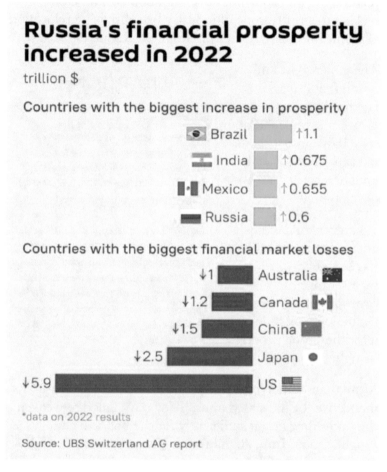

Russia's financial prosperity increased in 2022

trillion $

Countries with the biggest increase in prosperity

Brazil	↑1.1
India	↑0.675
Mexico	↑0.655
Russia	↑0.6

Countries with the biggest financial market losses

↓1	Australia
↓1.2	Canada
↓1.5	China
↓2.5	Japan
↓5.9	US

*data on 2022 results

Source: UBS Switzerland AG report

Sanctions were intended to destroy the Russian economy. It hasn't worked out that way. Russian government spending under Putin has always been rigorously managed. External debt per capita is just $2,352 per Russian, compared to $73,822 for each American. Growth and employment are robust. Russia became the first state to run a fiscal surplus after a year of war.

Sprinter ✓
@Sprinter99800

German Chancellor Olaf Scholz and French President Emmanuel Macron were surprised that Russian President Vladimir Putin during a telephone conversation on March 4, 2022, did not show the reaction to sanctions that the West expected, writes "Bild" .

"Something worries me more than the negotiations: Putin does not complain about the sanctions at all. I don't know if he did that in the conversation with you. But he didn't even mention them," the paper reports, quoting the words of Scholz in a conversation with his French colleague. Scholz also complained that Putin is only interested in reaching a compromise on the Ukrainian issue, especially on the demilitarization and denazification of Ukraine, the paper says.

15:06 · 28/08/2023 from Earth · **620K** Views

1,598 Reposts **123** Quotes **5,856** Likes **200** Bookmarks

Germany's fate was sealed with the explosion of the Nord Stream pipelines. Factory closures and bankruptcies are hollowing out the former economic titan of Europe. The German industrial and export model depended on wage and energy stability, and Germany has lost both. Investment is leaving. Germany's self-harm was increased by a determination to close low cost, reliable nuclear power plants. As predicted, the US has taken advantage of the crisis in Europe to restore the Rust Belt, although more production investment has migrated to China.

The US rose to be the global top exporter of oil and liquid natural gas as Europe cut ties with lower cost Russia and scrambled for other suppliers. LNG demand destruction and more reasonable policies may render US gains temporary.

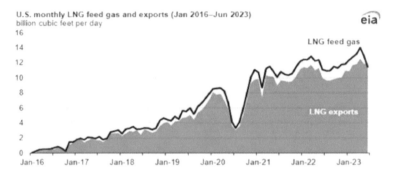

U.S. monthly LNG feed gas and exports (Jan 2016–Jun 2023)
billion cubic feet per day

The very last fertiliser plant in the UK has announced its closure as production is no longer economic with higher cost US and Norwegian gas. This will impact UK food production costs and inflation in the longer term.

Perhaps the most tragic loss arising from the sanctions on Russia is the abandonment of Western legal norms of rule of law, equal protection, non-discriminatory commercial law, due process, proximity to harm or causation, and reputation for fair dealing. These are essential to foreign investor confidence and cross-border commercial contract.

Abandonment of rule of law in the UK is particularly tragic for the City of London as the global financial capital. The UK had few comparative advantages left after Brexit, and the City provides a huge contribution to UK fiscal revenues.

Non-discriminatory rule of law in the City goes back to Roman times. It was reinforced by the 1066 Charter of London's Liberties from King William the Conqueror that accorded *Angli et Franci* burgesses of London equal liberties, rights, and protections. The turmoil in Westminster as prime ministers Johnson and Truss were forced out of office added to a global perception of UK lawlessness and chaos. Confidence has not been restored by a Sunak record of no-bid crony contracts and subsidies to firms in which his family or political donors have interests. A crisis in the gilts market started with broad, sustained foreign selling in August 2022, spiked with unwise fiscal laxity under Truss in September, and continues with gilts rates higher now than during the Truss market dysfunction.

Price Value Partners @PriceVPartners · 16h · · ·
Inflationary impact of Covid-related government spending means it makes sense to limit or eliminate exposure to UK **Gilts**. #valueinvesting. Read - Which lie did they tell ? bit.ly/3UlzpOP

IT STILL MAKES SENSE TO LIMIT OR ELIMINATE YOUR EXPOSURE TO UK GILTS.

0:01

ill 41

Not content with war on one continent, and permanent economic harm to one set of allies, the US has escalated a campaign of economic and commercial sanctions against China and Chinese companies that hurts allies in Asia. The lawlessness and breadth of US commercial sanctions have appalled many who appreciate the traditions and norms of non-discriminatory commercial law and principles of free trade. The veneer of 'security' concerns fools no one. The West is being out-competed as China's scientific and technical innovations and industrial primacy leave competitors trailing.

The chips and fabrication sanctions intended to deny China high tech advances will result in huge damage to those states unwise enough to bow to US pressure. Exports are falling in Japan, Korea, Taiwan, and will soon fall in the Netherlands as Chinese companies substitute domestic production to ensure security of supply and resiliency.

US commercial sanctions have led to a wholesale reorientation of the Chinese economy from infrastructure- and housing- as drivers of growth to technology and Artificial Intelligence (AI) for a new industrial revolution. AI in China is used 90% for corporate efficiency and industrial production gains, and the rate of process improvement is accelerating.

Rebecca Chan
@RebeccaYChan

...

"Huawei Cloud CEO Zhang Pingan...with a dismissive nod to ChatGPT: "The Pangu model does not compose poetry, nor does it have time to compose poetry, because its job is to go deep into all walks of life, and help AI add value to all walks of life."

9:13 AM · Sep 4, 2023 · **317** Views

Huawei leads the world in telecommunications technology, research and development, and there is no Western peer of the same quality or cost. The US attempt to sanction Huawei out of existence or into a US listing has not worked but has caused real harm to China-US relations.

The Canadian arrest of CFO Wanzhou Meng at the request of US National Security Advisor John Bolton in December 2018 was particularly ill-judged. The US fabricated charges of dealing with Iran and

bank fraud using a slide deck leaked by Huawei's bank. Huawei had previously refused to license its technologies to US rivals or to list on US exchanges, angering US corporate and investment elites who could not otherwise compete or profit from Huawei's global rise and technological superiority. The US was also angered by denial of access and backdoors for US intelligence and surveillance now customary in allied telecommunications technologies.

Charges were dropped after three years of Meng's house arrest in Vancouver. Huawei remains 100% owned by its employees and pensioners. Anger at US and Canadian injustice made all staff more motivated to remove foreign technology dependencies. Other Chinese companies have also taken defensive measures to reduce foreign supplier risks.

Meng's arrest continued a pattern of executive harassment to gain advantage for US rivals or asset managers. The 2013 arrest of Frédéric Pierucci, CEO of Alstom, on charges of corruption, led to a 2 year imprisonment. Alstom was forced to pay the biggest ever penalty and cede control of some units to General Electric, its US rival. Pierucci's book, *The American Trap*, details how the US uses sanctions, regulations, and corporate law as economic weaponry to destabilise the world's largest companies to benefit US

rivals and asset managers. Since 2008 more than 30 corporations have paid fines above $100 million to the US Treasury. 16 are European, for more than $6 billion. The 7 American firms paying fines, paid an average third as much. US allies are particularly vulnerable, as they generally will not resist predatory targeting of their industries and cooperate with executive extraditions.

The Meng arrest and standoff led to tectonic shifts in global technology alignment that will affect growth globally for decades. The US constrained its allies to go along with bans on Huawei in telecoms and infrastructure. Inferior, more expensive, and more vulnerable alternatives render allies at risk of US surveillance, but also weaken competitiveness, spur inflation, and drive offshoring in their economies.

UK rose to primacy in global banking, financial services, and FinTech largely because British Telecom was a first mover in total replacement modernisation of broadband and mobile infrastructure in the 1990s. BT was Huawei's first foreign customer. It is now hard to imagine how backward and uncompetitive UK would be had BT remained with the venerable Marconi. UK kept pace over two decades with rapid Huawei network improvements, including nationwide rollout of highspeed fibre broadband to businesses and households and 4G. BT and mobile network operators will be forced to remove Huawei fibre and components from networks before a government-imposed 2027 deadline, creating uncertainty on network adequacy, adding huge replacement costs, and further discouraging domestic and foreign investment dependent on 5G infrastructure.

US, UK, and other allies who have banned Huawei will soon lag even poor developing countries that benefit from superior Huawei 5G, 5.5G and 6G infrastructure, private 5G and AI industrialisation, Cloud, Web 3.0, satellite, data storage, and industrial and commercial AI innovations. It is a self-inflicted wound that will only fester as Huawei continues to innovate and globalise its technologies.

Huawei's most celebrated revenge came as US Secretary of Commerce Gina Raimondo visited Beijing 30 August 2023. Raimondo convinced TSMC to ban the sale of its 5G chips to Huawei in 2019, just as China was switching nationwide to 5G. The move was intended to destroy Huawei's smartphone business; it reduced Huawei smartphone sales by 90%.

Huawei chose the day Secretary Raimondo negotiated commerce in Beijing to put its first new 5G phone – with 100% Chinese parts and a new domestically produced Kirin 9000S chip – on unannounced sale in shops and online. The chip is so advanced the phone is 5G, 5.5G and satellite for places with no cell signal. The HarmonyOS operating system was internally developed by Huawei after sanctions denied Google Android. Satellite connectivity supplements 5G. Download speeds are the fastest among peers. The Mate 60 Pro sold out within hours, despite official announcement scheduled for 12 September.

Secretary Raimondo has spearheaded hundreds of commercial sanctions against Chinese companies, but now wants to reopen trade talks. The irony wasn't lost on Chinese. The timing of the Mate 60 Pro release echoed the test flight of the J-20, a fifth-generation stealth fighter, during the 2012 visit of US Defence Secretary Robert Gates (former Deputy Director of the CIA in the Cold War).

In a hopeful sign, the sanctions tide may be turning. Iran recently succeeded in securing return of $6 billion official reserves frozen since 1979 at the New York Fed and has doubled oil exports to 2 million barrels daily. Similarly the US has encouraged Chevron to increase Venezuelan oil production and exports.

Tensions remain. The US Navy has seized two Iranian oil tankers, diverting them to US ports for sale of oil.

Unilateral sanctions are already discouraged or barred in the United Nations Charter, a key resolution of the New International Economic Order, and as a principle of the BRICS+ cooperating states.

Sanctions don't work, hurt the sanctioned as much as the

sanctioner, create inflationary added costs, and fan global distrust and uncertainty that discourages foreign investment and commerce. State and non-state actors will decide for themselves who they do business with and what business is in their mutual interest, and they will protect that business from seizure, foreign dependencies, foreign interference, and sanctions risks. The West can align with a shift away from unilateral sanctions or be left behind.

↻ Arnaud Bertrand reposted

Arnaud Bertrand ✓ @RnaudBertrand · 12h
Replying to @Lularcdcn

Ask yourself one question: if de-risking were about supply chain resilience, why is it aimed solely at China? Why not say "critical industries like pharmaceuticals should be produced at home"? Because it ain't about resilience but about decoupling from China...

◯ 1   ↻ 6   ♡ 65   ⅈⅼⅈ 2,358   ⬆

Dr. Anglo Phd 🌑
@Ken04989139

📧 We need to destroy Huawei(H)
H: why ?
📧 Because we can
📧 No you can't
📧 Arrests Meng
📧 Detains the two Micheals
📧 You can't do that
📧 Yes we can
📧 Sanction Huawei
H: builds better chips
📧 You can't do that
📧 Yes we can.
📧 It's not fair we were supposed to win
📧 No you weren't

01:06 · 03/09/2023 · **13.7K** Views

Kathleen Tyson ✓
@Kathleen_Tyson_

···

Angell Paradox: Every Asian state that signed up for chip sanctions and new US missile bases since October 2022 is seeing exports collapse. China will avert World War 3 by making it unaffordable.

🐼 **ShanghaiPanda** @thinking_panda · Jul 14
Korea's exports drop 14.8 percent in the first 10 days of July... Monthly exports have been on a declining trend for the past nine consecutive months, starting from October last year... semiconductor exports dropped by 36.8 percent compared with a year ago.
m.pulsenews.co.kr/view.php?year=...

| Biz | Bio&Tech | Market | Economy | > |

Korea's exports drop 14.8 percent in the first 10 days of July

2023.07.11 13:36:02   2023.07.11 13:48:18

A- A+

11:18 AM · Jul 14, 2023 · **78.4K** Views

7 RESILIENCY, STABILITY AND INFLATION

Siasi King
@KingSiasi

· · ·

IMF Managing Director #Kristalina_Georgieva **On How Trade Using**
#Local_Currencies **Can Help Emerging Economies.**

4:57 AM · Sep 3, 2023 · **29** Views

A United Nations Resolution on a New International
Economic Order (NIEO) has passed regularly since the first
in 1974. Now for the first time the BRICS+ and global East
and South are collectively implementing many aspirations
of the NIEO among themselves. Cooperation among state
and non-state actors are improving resiliency, stability, and
control of inflation that promote collective prosperity.

The map of the NIEO vote is the West vs the Rest. 123 states, 64% of UN member states, with more than 7 billion in population favoured NIEO. States aligned with the West opposed. Turkiye abstained.

The institutions driving change are now clearer: Belt and Road Initiative (BRI) builds infrastructure that draws inward investment and grows jobs and fiscal capacity; Asian Infrastructure and Investment Bank (AIIB) provides a multilateral institution for financing infrastructure-led development where the members have far more influence than they ever did in Bretton Woods institutions; and BRICS+ promotes dynamic bilateral cooperation matching need with proven capacity for joint ventures.

UN General Assembly Vote on Item 20 -A/77/445 DR
Date: 14-Dec-2022
Topic: Towards a new international economic order

The NIEO Resolution:

- Reaffirms "the need to continue working towards a new international economic order based on the principles of equity, sovereign equality, interdependence, common interest, cooperation and solidarity among all States."

- Reiterates "that States are strongly urged to refrain from promulgating and applying any unilateral economic, financial or trade measures not in accordance with international law and the Charter of the United Nations that impede the full achievement of economic and social development, particularly in developing countries."

- Calls for "mutually supporting world trade, monetary and financial systems" and "coordination of macroeconomic policies among countries to avoid negative spillover effects, especially in developing countries."

- Urges debt relief, "expresses concern over the increasing debt vulnerabilities of developing countries, the net negative capital flows from developing countries, the fluctuation of exchange rates and the tightening of global financial conditions, and in this regard stresses the need to explore the means and instruments needed to achieve debt sustainability and the measures necessary to reduce the indebtedness of developing countries."

BRICS formed as a forum of Brazil, Russia, India, China, and South Africa in 2010. 'BRIC' as an acronym was coined by Goldman Sachs economist Jim O'Neill to describe the fast-growing economies that would dominate global growth to 2050. Adding Argentina, Egypt, Ethiopia, Iran, Saudi Arabia, and United Arab Emirates at the August 2023 meeting in South Africa, BRICS+ is becoming a significant forum for global South cooperation and development.

NIEO aspirations are repeated in the Declaration released on the final day of the BRICS+ XV Summit in South

Africa. The difference is that BRICS+ delivers a series of bilateral deals and investments worth hundreds of billions that will drive faster change and growth.

Sidelining the bureaucracy and institutional process of multilateral institutions is a huge win for the developing world. It is much faster to identify an opportunity, identify a partner to meet the need, and move forward under jointly agreed terms and financing. BRICS+ is still new, still evolving, but the action happens less in the summit than in the side meetings that announce new bilateral deals.

Resiliency is the property of withstanding an economic or financial shock without large or persistent losses. Under the Bretton Woods system emerging markets were never resilient. Every inflationary or economic shock hit the poor more than the rich, hit the weakest hardest, and they recovered much more slowly than G7. The poor and weak almost never recovered pre-shock trend growth.

Often forced by crisis to borrow or enforce austerity, poor states become more fiscally constrained by debt service, unable to fund adequate education, healthcare, and infrastructure that would attract inward investment. Aid and debt have never yet lifted a country out of poverty into prosperous development.

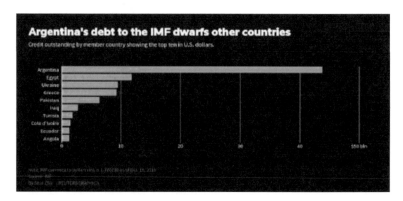

A look at the top 10 IMF creditors tells its own story. Most are serial borrowers, using the next IMF programme to service interest payments on past borrowings. The Bretton Woods institutions will continue, but effective development is rapidly shifting to alternative methods.

It makes sense for the global South to self-organise its own development going forward. Surplus states invest in poorer states, growing their capacity and sharing models for success.

- Global East and South are driving over 80 percent of global growth in GDP, up from just 20 percent in the 1990s;
- Global East and South are now huge sources of development finance and foreign direct investment, with China the largest investor through BRI, bilateral aid, and corporate foreign direct investment;
- Global East and South private sector companies are increasingly looking at expansion opportunities in their regions or Africa, driving local engagement, growth in capacity, and employment;
- Identifying latent comparative advantage and underexploited resources is more effectively accomplished through direct and dynamic engagement than remote analytics or economics;
- As its industries move up the value chain, China will upskill and re-locate low-skill jobs, management, and fiscal capacity to poorer states.

Each BRICS+ nation brings a different set of resources, finances, skills, experience, capacity, and comparative advantage. Any country can be a recipient or a contributor to bilateral project finance.

Western observers tend to dismiss BRICS+ for not having a charter, a headquarters, management hierarchy, rules, or membership criteria. They miss the point entirely. BRICS+ is stronger without those trappings of institutional rigidity because in BRICS+ every state and non-state actor has agency to get things done with anyone who agrees the deal. BRICS+ is dynamic, agile, adaptive.

Some say BRICS+ will be unstable because there are no shared political systems or values, and even some border disputes and historic animosity (e.g., India and China). BRICS+ restores a central role for Realpolitik to global diplomacy, eradicated by shared-values and ideological purges in Western diplomatic corps. Realpolitik diplomacy looks for shared interest in deliverable outcomes, ignores political differences, historical conflict, 'values', and labels.

It helps to think of BRICS+ as *holacratic*, entirely without hierarchy or bureaucracy. Holacracy is a method of decentralised management and organisational governance where all actors have agency, authority, and decision-making. It is derivative of the Greek *holons* or ὅλον meaning 'whole', and signifies that units are sovereign, autonomous, and self-reliant, but also dependent on the greater whole of which they are parts. Within BRICS+ every state is sovereign and equal, hence no rules, and every state and non-state actor in BRICS+ decides and acts for itself, guided by its own interests. They act independently but share wider goals and aspirations for shared progress.

It is up to every BRICS+ state and non-state actor to dynamically identify partnership opportunities of mutual interest and benefit and agree bilaterally any investment and terms. Distributed decision-making is better suited to a complex, rapidly changing world which desperately needs dynamism and innovation. Rules and institutional bureaucracy would only add uncertainty, costs, and delays.

The list of deals coming out of the recent BRICS XV Summit is impressive in number, scope, and scale of ambition:

- A Chinese contractor will build a new airport in Tehran with AI assisted cargo logistics capacity in exchange for oil shipments, circumventing sanctions on the sale of Iranian oil;
- 5 Iranian-built oil refineries in energy-poor South Africa will promote export revenues and relieve a drain on foreign exchange;
- Brazil-Argentina will have a joint trade finance facility in yuan, leveraging Argentina's generous yuan swap line;
- China will build a nuclear power plant in Saudi to green the Saudi economy;
- China will modernise grid and generation capacity for crisis-hit South Africa, plagued with brown-outs from degraded grid and generation infrastructure;
- Iran-Iraq will barter of electricity for crude oil and mazut (fuel residue), side-lining the oft-frozen Iraqi oil revenues account at the New York Fed.

Past cooperation within BRICS+ are already paying off. The first freight train from Moscow to Saudi Arabia and India is in transit as I write. The North-South Corridor, first agreed in 2000, is 40 percent shorter and 30 percent less expensive than alternative sea routes. The Caspian Sea will soon be connected to the Persian Gulf and Indian Ocean through additional rail routes.

Sentletse
@Sentletse

Russia has sent first cargo to Saudi Arabia via Iran through the North-South Transport Corridor.

African needs its own North-South transport corridor to make the AfCFTA a reality. Without infrastructure in place and open borders (visa free), the implementation of AfCFTA will never happen.

9:06 AM · Aug 31, 2023 · 3,483 Views

China launched its own Belt and Road Initiative in 2013, which now reaches 155 nations, 75% of global population, and half of global GDP. BRI development combines aid, trade, and investment, and incorporates transparency, accountability, and selectivity. China developed its own

economy on similar lines, so there is enthusiasm in BRI partners to do what is proven effective. BRI combines regional cooperation, trade, tariff reductions, and transport efficiency for long-term economic transformation.

The scale of infrastructure already delivered – highways, railways, bridges, tunnels, hydroelectric dams, hospitals, universities, and more – is stunning. Laos, the most bombed nation on Earth, landlocked and poor, now has a high-speed railway combining passenger and freight that interlinks with China's rail network. Belt and Road trade has grown rapidly, to the point where BRI as a group now trade more with China than ASEAN, EU, and US combined.

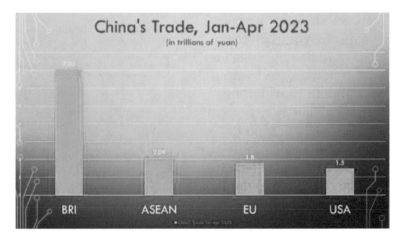

The next signal event was the founding of the Asian Infrastructure Investment Bank, founded in 2015 with 57 members. Shanghai-based AIIB adapted China's bilateral cooperation on infrastructure to a multilateral institution for regional and global reach. AIIB now has 107 members, 47 within the Asian region and 45 more globally. China and others had tried for decades to reform the Bretton Woods institutions, only to meet with frustration and ever more debt with conditionality. Starting afresh on better principles was simpler and faster.

Cooperation among BRICS+ and aligned states on energy, food, and development will change resiliency, stability, and inflation dynamics. China and Russia both lead in power generation technologies, logistics, and agricultural productivity optimisation, but with different technologies and skillsets. Both were net importers of food 20 years ago, and both are self-sufficient or exporters today.

Reforms to agriculture will contribute greatly to improved resiliency and stability in the global South. China has 1.4 billion population but just 0.08 hectare arable land per capita, a mere 7 percent of global arable land. Only10 percent of China's vast land is suitable for cultivation. Food self-sufficiency has been a priority since trade embargoes and blockades caused widespread famine in the 1950s. China's food production strategy is technology-led, with soil surveys every five years analysed against crop yields at a granular level nationwide. The analysis has multiple uses. Farmers can better understand when to fertilise, plant, weed, treat for pests, and harvest. Shared reporting improves planning each year. Planning authorities identify where canals, irrigation pipes and trenches, or other agricultural infrastructure can improve production. AI is increasingly integrated with monitoring, spraying, and harvesting to optimise yields. These methods can be shared widely in the global South to improve food self-sufficiency.

Despite technical self-sufficiency being achieved, China remains the world's largest food importer. This provides a basis for cooperation in broader food production, particularly in Africa. It is an unspeakable tragedy that Africa is not self-sufficient in food. States have the capacity to grow rapidly with better agricultural policies, technologies, and investment. In 2023 food cooperation is scaling rapidly as the food price shock from dollarised inflation and war in Ukraine spurred new policies.

Ethiopia is a model of what longer term Chinese cooperation brings. One of the earliest countries to partner with China in the Belt and Road Initiative, Ethiopia has seen rapid and stable real GDP growth near 10 percent since 2010. Sesame seeds and coffee are among the biggest export crops, with 60-70 percent shipped to China. This export market consistency provides stability to Ethiopia's fiscal capacity. Ethiopia has the lowest debt arrears as a percent of GDP of any Sub-Saharan African nation, with the highest and most stable GDP growth. Ethiopia can be a model for China's infrastructure-led and technology-led development in EMDE partners.

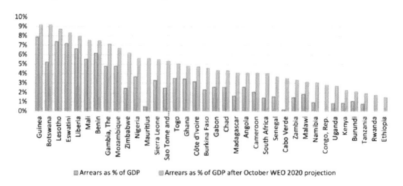

112

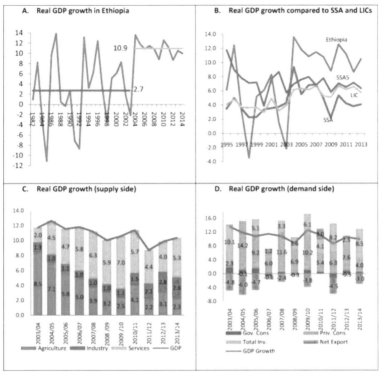

Moller, L.C. and Wacker, K., Explaining Ethiopia's Growth Acceleration – The Role of Infrastructure and Macroeconomic Policy, World Development (August 2017), Vol. 96, pp 198-215, https://doi.org/10.1016/j.worlddev.2017.03.007.

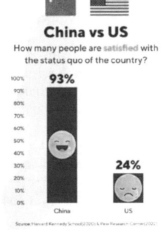

Cooperation among BRICS+ partners and other states on electrification and telecommunications is particularly critical to sustained economic progress. Electricity usage is highly correlated to industrialisation and GDP per capita. Both Russia and China are engaging with global South to build electricity and telecommunications capacity that will transform the poorest economies.

Electricity & Income (per capita, all countries)

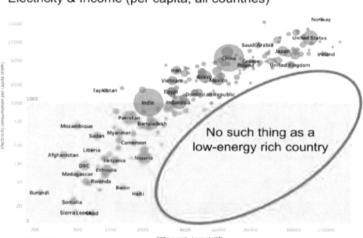

Source: IEA, World Bank

Inflation is a challenge globally in the wake of the pandemic and war in Ukraine. Here again different models of economic and monetary management may be suitable, beyond those taught in Western universities. Russia and China have nationwide price monitoring systems covering thousands of items that alert central banks and policy makers to rising prices, regionally or nationally. Authorities can investigate whether price rises are due to shortages, supply chain problems, profiteering, or localised conditions. Interventions to resolve the drivers of inflation can bring inflation down more quickly than remote and uncertain transmission via monetary policies and financial institutions.

China also stockpiles energy, commodities, and food to relieve shortages immediately they are identified. This supply chain resiliency enabled China to keep inflation low in 2022, peaking at 3.4 percent, as inflation in developed countries spiked sharply higher, often into double digits. Monetary policy is ill-adapted to supply-driven inflation. Diversity of methods – and shared experience – may be more relevant to managing inflationary shocks than monetary modelling.

enrico @enrico221960 · 2d
As a Kenyan official put it: Every time China visits we get a hospital, every time Britain visits we get a lecture.

♡ 317   ⟲ 6,174   ♡ 33.7K   ⤴

Mark Seddon @MarkSeddon1962 · 1d
Replying to @enrico221960
Maybe, but how will Kenya be obliged to pay this investment back? No such thing as a free hospital?

♡ 57   ⟲ 16   ♡ 191   ⤴

reegs
@stillreezy

Replying to @MarkSeddon1962 and @enrico221960

here comes the lecture lol

1:22 · 26 Mar 22 · Twitter for iPhone

108A ...
@108SAR

TO BETTER UNDERSTAND
AMERICAN ENGLISH
Brilliant definitions! By @ricwe123

🌟"Democracies" are those states in which the US has managed to overthrow or install a client regime.

🌟"Authoritarian regimes" are countries where the US has not yet been successful in doing so.

3:40 PM · May 14, 2023 · **1,531** Views

8 GOLD RETURNS

"Gold is a currency. It is still, by all evidence, a premier currency, where no fiat currency, including the dollar, can match it."

- Alan Greenspan, Council on Foreign Relations, October 2014

Gold has been a hegemonic asset for settlement of interstate debts and payment of imperial tribute since the earliest empires discovered metallurgy to refine gold and silver from ore. Wherever they conquered, empires demanded tribute and payment in gold and silver. As nation states evolved, the strong still conquered the weak and demanded tribute paid in gold for trade, war reparations, and imperial 'protection'. Germany's World War I reparations were paid in gold. Lend-Lease payments were in gold too. Britain had more gold than the US at the start of the World War II, but by its end its gold had shipped westwards never to return. By 1945 the US had 80 percent of all gold reserves.

Gold ceased its role as a hegemonic asset for interstate settlements when the US unilaterally repudiated its Bretton Woods dollars-for-gold exchange obligation in 1971. Too much gold was being demanded for shipment east as US wartime deficits surged.

The world has since had floating fiat currencies, trading against dollar for the most part. We've also seen unanchored expansion of debt, inflation, wage stagnation, and periodic financial crisis. Workers have endured decades of lower than trend wage growth under policies that promote corporate and elite low taxation. A reversion to gold as a monetary base will likely lead to wider reforms in economic and fiscal policies.

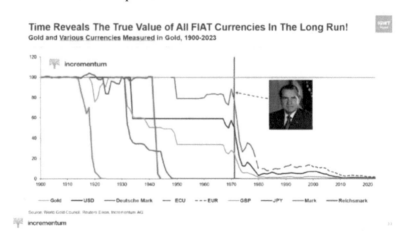

Time Reveals The True Value of All FIAT Currencies In The Long Run!
Gold and Various Currencies Measured in Gold, 1900-2023

Productivity & Real Incomes Are Still Drifting Further Apart

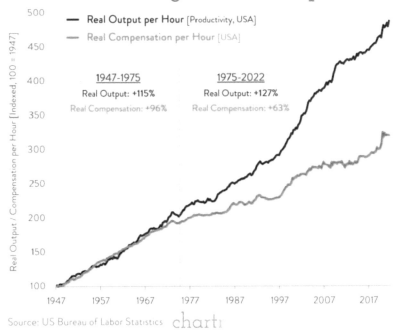

Source: US Bureau of Labor Statistics   charti

Gold Is Up YTD in every Currency and Outperforms Most Domestic Stock Indices
Gold in Local Currency, and Domestic Stock Index, Annual Performance in %, 2023 YTD

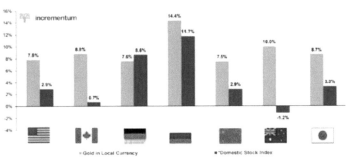

incrementum

The benefits of gold as an alternative hegemonic asset include:

- **Scarcity:** The global supply of gold is limited, purity is assayable, so it cannot be easily debased;
- **Durability:** Gold is durable and does not decay (although ingots have to be periodically shifted or they meld together);
- **Portability:** Gold can be transported and stored locally and does not rely on a payment system;
- **Divisibility:** Gold can be divided into smaller units, so offers a store of value to less well off as well as wealthy elites, often bought as jewellery;
- **Convertibility:** Gold can be traded for currency or oil, less so for goods, but offers a valid medium of exchange in most parts of the world;
- **Security:** Gold in self-custody has no counterparty or custody risk that is not under direct, local control.

The era of fiat central banks has been chaotic and disappointing. Growth has slowed. Wages have suffered. Instability has increased with leverage and financialisation replacing savings and industrialisation. As Paul Volcker, former Chairman of the Federal Reserve Board of Governors, observed:

> "If is a sobering fact that the prominence of central banks in this century has coincide with a general tendency towards more inflation, not less. If the overriding objective is price stability, we did better with the nineteenth-century gold standard and passive central banks, with currency boards, or even with 'free banking'. The truly unique power of a central bank, after all, is the power to create money, and ultimately the power to create is the power to destroy."

Perhaps the greatest advantage of gold is that the world agrees on gold, even when they can agree on little else. Gold doesn't care about your values or politics and is simple enough to weigh rather than model. The BRICS have been discussing alternatives since forming in 2009, but there is no agreement. Meanwhile central banks are buying record amounts of gold in 2023. Viewed pragmatically, gold is what we agree on.

The institutions of the 20th century were founded with gold as the hegemonic asset for interstate settlements, so could adjust if gold returns. The Bank for International Settlements was conceived and founded in 1930 by three US mercantile banks to simplify the logistics of gold settlements in Europe, and particularly payment of German war reparations in gold. BIS initial capital amounted to five hundred million gold-backed Swiss francs (145,162,290.32 grammes fine gold).

The Bretton Woods Treaty institutions were all backed by gold. The World Bank was founded with gold endowments from its founding stakeholders. The International Monetary Fund was founded to underpin Bretton Woods Treaty fixed convertibility of currencies into gold for the promotion of wider trade and credit. The gold-backed US dollar globalised price quotations in dollars, but by extension gold as well. $35 dollars per ounce, a rate set by President Roosevelt in 1933, became the basis for the Bretton Woods Treaty from 1944 and provided global price stability until 1971.

Gold purchases by central banks were higher in 2022 than any year since 1968. The gold purchases have accelerated in the first quarter of 2023, reaching new record levels.

The Peoples' Bank of China, long silent on gold, started announcing monthly accumulations in late 2022, publicly signalling with its own actions a preference for gold over foreign exchange accumulation. Other central banks are becoming more forthright about gold accumulation as well.

There is no agreement on what gold means, or how it will be used yet from officials or multilateral institutions, but clearly gold is part of the New International Economic Order.

Whether the BRICS+ will have a gold-linked currency was a source of recent controversy, settled by inaction at the BRICS XV Summit. More likely is a system of gold convertibility of among BRICS currencies. Shanghai Gold Exchange allows CNY conversion to gold for export. Moscow Gold Exchange allows RUB conversion to gold for export. South Africa has always exported monetary gold. UAE, a new member from January 2021, has a very active gold exchange.

All BRICS have significant gold reserves as of July 2023:

- **Brazil** has the 10th largest gold reserves in the world, with 123.4 metric tons.
- **Russia** has the 6th largest gold reserves in the world, with 2,300 metric tons.
- **India** has the 5th largest gold reserves in the world, with 757.2 metric tons.
- **China** has the 3rd largest gold reserves in the world, with 1,948.3 metric tons.
- **South Africa** has the 11th largest gold reserves in the world, with 125.2 metric tons.

A new gold-backed currency has been mooted, but some scepticism is warranted. Any commodity-linked currency eventually gets abused and debased by the powerful or by insiders, just as the gold-backed dollar was abused and debased by the United States only 5 years after the creation of the Federal Reserve and 100% gold backing of the dollar. The decades-long manipulations of gold pricing in existing financialised markets for gold are well known. Further, without periodic accounting, audits, and assays it is impossible to know if the gold reported as reserves is really in custody. Even if it is there, as with US repudiation in 1971, holders may find they are refused when they seek gold from the depository.

Large Western banks and central banks which too freely borrowed or swapped gold in the past have a vested collective interest in manipulating the price of gold lower. A record of 'spoofing' and 'wash trading' among major banks is an old story. The gold price manipulation was conducted with central bank silence, if not active support. Like Libor rate rigging, central bankers may also rig gold markets when it suits them.

Jack Straw @JackStr42679640 · Sep 3
SPOOFING!!!

finance.yahoo.com
Ex-JPMorgan Gold Traders Get Prison for 'Prolific Spoofing'
(Bloomberg) -- The former head of JPMorgan Chase & Co.'s precious-metals desk and his top trader were sentenced to prison for spoofing,...

12   21   1,614

classicalliberty
@jsolom100

Not sure who needs to hear this, but the Gold standard was much better for workers.

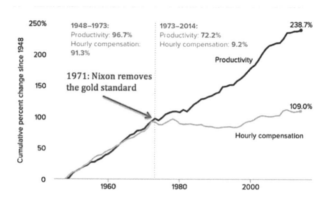

Note: Data are for average hourly compensation of production/nonsupervisory workers in the private sector and net productivity of the total economy. "Net productivity" is the growth of output of goods and services minus depreciation per hour worked.

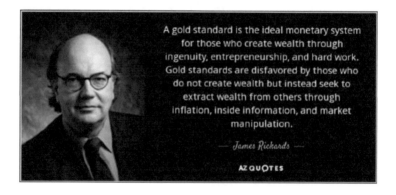

A gold standard is the ideal monetary system for those who create wealth through ingenuity, entrepreneurship, and hard work. Gold standards are disfavored by those who do not create wealth but instead seek to extract wealth from others through inflation, inside information, and market manipulation.

— James Rickards —

AZ QUOTES

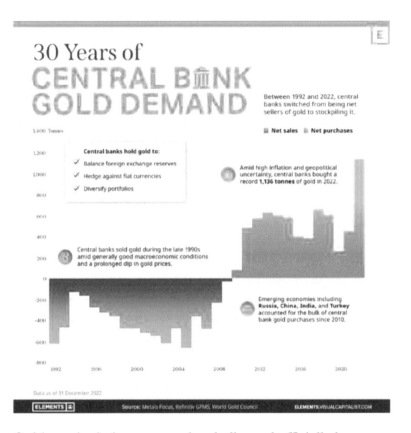

30 Years of
CENTRAL B🏛NK
GOLD DEMAND

Between 1992 and 2022, central banks switched from being net sellers of gold to stockpiling it.

1,400 Tonnes

■ Net sales ■ Net purchases

Central banks hold gold to:
✓ Balance foreign exchange reserves
✓ Hedge against fiat currencies
✓ Diversify portfolios

Amid high inflation and geopolitical uncertainty, central banks bought a record **1,136 tonnes** of gold in 2022.

Central banks sold gold during the late 1990s amid generally good macroeconomic conditions and a prolonged dip in gold prices.

Emerging economies including **Russia, China, India,** and **Turkey** accounted for the bulk of central bank gold purchases since 2010.

Data as of 31 December 2022

ELEMENTS   Source: Metals Focus, Refinitiv GFMS, World Gold Council   ELEMENTS.VISUALCAPITALIST.COM

Gold manipulations cannot be challenged officially because it would require admitting that the most secret gold swaps happened, and it would require cross-border cooperation in a global market to stabilise currencies. If Western banks were ever required to restore swapped gold to official reserves at central banks, it would be at much higher prices than when borrowed, now near $2000 per ounce, threatening their capital, solvency, global dominance, and systemic financial stability.

I know one European central bank that swapped out its gold reserves to Drexel Burnham Lambert prior to Drexel's insolvency in 1990. Drexel's losses and collateral calls on its massive gold swap book were a major factor in Drexel's failure. I was the New York Fed expert on swaps. I was asked to explain to a shaking and ashen central banker flown hurriedly to New York that he would not recover the central bank's gold in the insolvency resolution. His central bank still reports the gold as held on its balance sheet as if it were in custody, never publicly realising the loss.

Gold swaps are among the most secret of central bank transactions. There was anger, approaching panic, when a mere mention of gold swaps made it into the minutes of the Federal Open Market Committee in 1995. The mention is searchable, and I have now found it. In particular, the minutes were deemed indiscreet and resented not only because they admit gold swaps were transacted, but also discuss the Exchange Stabilization Fund (ESF) as a means of clandestine interventions to secretly finance or bribe foreign governments to align with US policies and stabilise currency and asset markets.

In response to a 2009 Freedom of Information Act request for information about gold swaps, a Federal Reserve board member replied by letter that gold swaps would not be disclosed to the public under an exemption for Federal Reserve Bank operations. The sensitivity around gold and gold swaps means no official reporting or accounting is any longer reliable.

Officially the US remains the largest holder of gold in the world. US Treasury official gold reserves in Fort Knox have not been audited since the early 1960s. No one knows what we would find there today.

MR. TRUMAN. Yes. They have made loans to or financial arrangements with at least 37 countries around the world over the last 50 years.

MR. LINDSEY. I think we all will be asked questions about this. Can you read this paper and tell me that there is not something missing that I should know about, meaning that this is not only the truth but the whole truth?

MR. TRUMAN. I can only say that Treasury lawyers have looked into the question of whether these operations are legal under this broad authorization of what they can do and what the purpose is--

MR. MATTINGLY. If I can help out?

MR. LINDSEY. Yes.

MR. MATTINGLY. It's pretty clear that these ESF operations are authorized. I don't think there is a legal problem in terms of the authority. The statute is very broadly worded in terms of words like "credit"--it has covered things like the gold swaps--and it confers broad authority. Counsel at the White House called the Treasury's General Counsel today and asked "Are you sure?" And the Treasury's General Counsel said "I am sure." Everyone is satisfied that a legal issue is not involved, if that helps.

MR. LINDSEY. Is there anything missing on this page?

MR. MATTINGLY. No, there is not. If you look at the last paragraph, for example, that is part of the statute.

MR. LINDSEY. About notifying Congress in writing in advance?

MR. MATTINGLY. The statute says that with the permission of the President they can make loans.

MR. MELZER. In the penultimate paragraph, what is the identified source of repayment?

VICE CHAIRMAN MCDONOUGH. The Mexicans historically have been very sensitive about that. Now the whole world is informed that there are oil payments as an assured method of repayment. The Mexicans, for reasons with which you would be very familiar given Mexican history, have been rather sensitive about that being quite so open as it is now.

Exchanges for gold among BRICS will likely require pricing of gold move from London and New York to the East where gold is physically held and exchanged. Dubai is already a global centre for gold trading, and likely to become more important. Gold exchanges in Moscow and Shanghai provide a mechanism for exchanging currencies in closed economies – ruble and yuan – so these economies now integrate with global capital markets through gold without opening to foreign financial dominance and risks.

Gold will change perceptions of monetary policy if it becomes the reference for global value among enough states. Currency or commodity price in gold could become a reference for responsible governance again, and therefore a constraint on monetary and fiscal excesses.

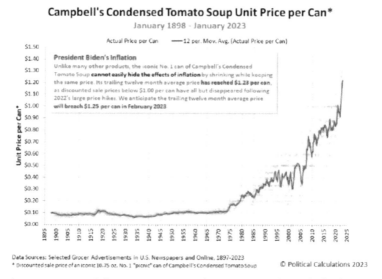

Campbell's Condensed Tomato Soup Unit Price per Can*
January 1898 - January 2023

Data Sources: Selected Grocer Advertisements in U.S. Newspapers and Online, 1897-2023
* Discounted sale price of an iconic 10.75 oz. No. 1 "picnic" can of Campbell's Condensed Tomato Soup

© Political Calculations 2023

A return to gold as a monetary base can reduce inflation, and that can improve growth recovery and resiliency during shocks. The graph above shows the price of a tin of Campbell's Tomato Soup stayed constant despite a financial mania in the 1920s, depression in the 1930s, and two world wars until the repudiation of the Bretton Woods Treaty in 1971. The price of soup has been volatile since as US monetary policy became increasingly erratic.

Gold's role in the global economy will be different from the Bretton Woods regime in one important way. The market price of gold – and by extension the gold price of any currency – are now determined on exchanges. Bretton Woods fixed the conversion price for currencies against gold, and this led to shocks as currencies were periodically devalued after periods of political or financial instability. With distributed centres of exchange-traded gold, currencies can rise and fall in gold terms, and relative to each other and gold. Gold exchanges are supplemental, not replacing foreign exchange markets.

Gold may change geostrategic alignments and security risks, something of continuing concern. Gold reserves disappeared from both Iraq and Libya during military aggressions against those nations, leaving them permanently poorer. If the US chooses to use its military to target foreign gold reserves, security around gold custody will need to strengthen in both allies and rivals, but particularly in smaller states with disproportionate wealth.

Many smaller states accumulating gold may not disclose gold reserves accurately to protect themselves from invasion and theft. Kazakhstan, where an attempted coup failed in January 2022, has large gold reserves. Had the coup been successful, perhaps their gold would be missing now, like Iraq and Libya's gold.

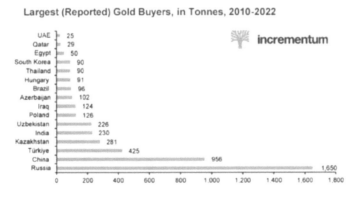

Largest (Reported) Gold Buyers, in Tonnes, 2010-2022

Source: World Gold Council, Incrementum AG

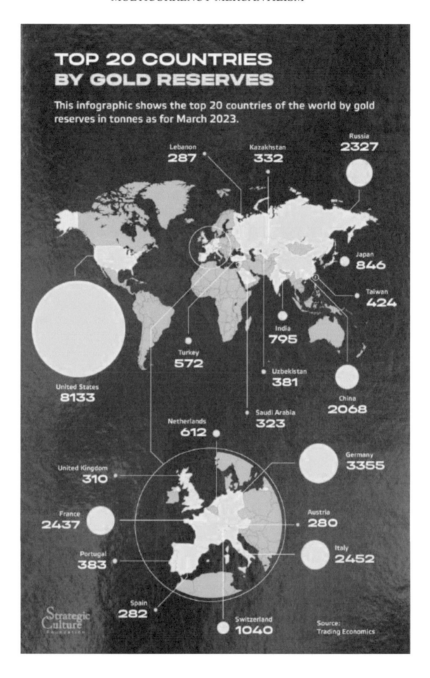

9 DEBT MANAGEMENT

The greatest transition challenge comes in management of the huge public and private debts. Global debt has grown more than 500% since 2000, and is now viewed by the United Nations, IMF, and World Bank as a global crisis affecting both developed and developing economies.

	Group of Seven							
Countries	Population	Annual GDP	GDP per capita	HDI	Debt ($M)	Debt (%GDP)	Deficit (%GDP)
Canada [+]	38,929,902	$1,988,336M	$52,015	0.929	2,243,918	112.85%	-5.04%
France [+]	67,842,582	$2,957,425M	$45,188	0.901	3,329,379	112.80%	-6.50%
Germany [+]	83,237,124	$4,262,767M	$51,238	0.947	2,968,690	68.60%	-3.70%
Italy [+]	58,983,122	$2,101,275M	$35,625	0.892	3,169,955	150.30%	-7.20%
Japan [+]	125,681,593	$4,932,556M	$39,246	0.919	13,053,658	259.43%	-8.97%
United Kingdom [+]	67,081,000	$3,186,860M	$47,508	0.932	3,039,338	95.35%	-7.99%
United States [+]	332,183,000	$23,315,100M	$69,227	0.926	29,463,730	128.13%	-10.91%
TOTAL: G7	773,938,323	$42,744,319M	$55,230		57,268,668	136.18%	

The challenge for the West is stark: The market for Western debt is contracting just as Western nations project higher unfunded deficits. Global accumulation of foreign exchange reserves peaked in 2021. Unilateral sanctions make foreigners wary of holding Western bonds as assets in 2022. Rapid rate hikes and bond write-downs in 2022-23 have further discouraged both domestic and foreign bond investment. Long-dated US Treasuries lost nearly half their value in just two years. And still the growth in US fiscal deficits accelerates, creating a potential global crisis in the global hegemonic currency and a disorderly reorientation to alternatives.

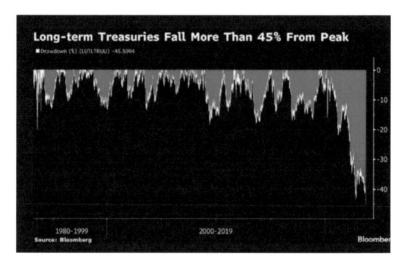

The accumulation of each other's debts as assets was never very well justified or rational. The practice started in 1922 with resolution 9 of the Genoa Convention to break the connection between major currencies and gold, allowing governments to issue debt as a supplemental form of money. Foreign balances in New York and London to 1929 seeded conditions for the speculative bubbles that burst in 1929. The World Bank and IMF promoted foreign exchange official reserves as good for 'financial stability' despite evidence being rather sketchy. Ever larger debts and US wars have repeatedly led to inflationary spikes, speculative excesses, and foreign exchange volatility. If the world is reconsidering whether to accumulate bonds or gold now, it should hardly surprise.

The transition to LCT and barter trade further erodes motivation to accumulate foreign exchange reserves. Western currencies are less important to LCT states' financial and economic stability and cooperation as they trade more with each other.

This leaves Western economies that continue to expand both trade and fiscal deficits in a bind. Unwilling to restore fiscal discipline, they must innovate new methods of financing ever higher debt. The US has reached $33.4 trillion in federal debt, 122% of GDP, and its own Treasury projections are for continued rapid debt escalation. The deficit has widened by $2 trillion in just the four months in 2023 since the debt ceiling was suspended by Congress. There is no budget, no audits, no controls on the speed of spending and debt escalation. It is a profoundly irresponsible fiscal policy from a country that proclaims leadership of the global order. Hardly surprising US is losing control of that order when it can no longer produce the books, much less balance the books.

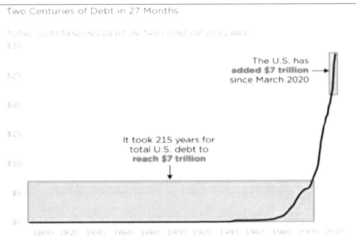

Two Centuries of Debt in 27 Months

TOTAL OUTSTANDING DEBT IN TRILLIONS OF DOLLARS

The U.S. has added $7 trillion since March 2020

It took 215 years for total U.S. debt to reach $7 trillion

From March 2020 to June 2022, a span of just 27 months, the federal government added $7 trillion to the national debt as a result of a massive spending spree. It took the government 215 years, from George Washington to George W. Bush, to initially reach $7 trillion in debt.

Fitch rating agency downgraded US Treasury debt in August 2023 to AA+ on 'expected fiscal deterioration', 'high and growing debt', and 'erosion of governance'. The attack on the Capitol in 2021, serial Debt Ceiling standoffs, and absence of any fiscal discipline are taking a toll on global and domestic confidence in Treasuries. Government spends more and delivers less for the nation every year as the US lags its peers on education, health, and many other indicators of good governance.

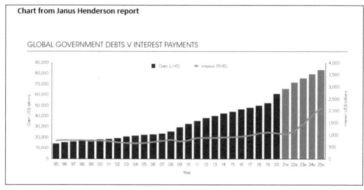

Chart from Janus Henderson report

GLOBAL GOVERNMENT DEBTS V INTEREST PAYMENTS

Benjamin Dietrich @DietrichBen · Aug 1

Fitch not unfairly downgrades US on 'erosion of **governance**' via @FT

ft.com

Fitch downgrades US on 'erosion of governance'

Fair enough!

♡ 1   ↻   ♡ 1   ılı 60

The State of the World's Government Debt

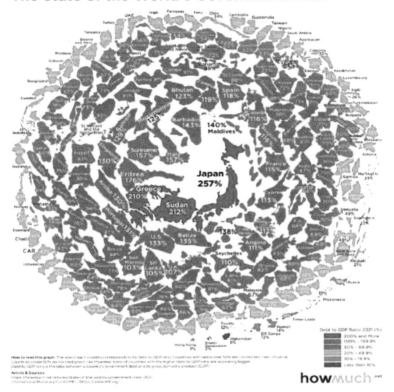

Fiscal dominance occurs when a central bank's efforts to fight inflation are compromised by decisions of the government. It's going to be a growing theme of monetary economics from now on. Higher interest rates drive higher funding costs in a vicious circle. Higher debt issuance at higher rates drives the value of existing bonds down, which causes higher rates still, which creates a spiral of instability.

If we were honest about financial regulation, which we rarely are, we would admit the IMF official reserves narratives, BIS Basel Accords on bank supervision, mandatory margin for OTC derivatives, mandatory clearing, etc. are all policies at least partially motivated to force holding more government bonds. These policies and regulations force the purchase and holding of sovereign debt as reserves, capital, or margin assets. Lately supervisors have been floating the idea of bringing hedge funds and asset managers into the regulatory corral, likely so they too can be forced to buy government debt as 'capital' for 'stability'.

Problematically, the more widely sovereign debt is held as it destabilises the greater the systemic risk. Unfortunately this is not a view that will ever be aired to the Financial Stability Board.

Another likely the solution is a Daisy Chain: West's central banks print money (stealth QE) to buy each other's debt to stabilise debt markets with the appearance of foreign demand. This cross-currency window dressing accumulates as official foreign exchange reserves, making the foreign official reserves narrative more robust. A Daisy Chain is difficult to confirm as it only shows in aggregate IMF reserves reporting and each central bank's own published foreign official reserve reports.

% of US Treasury Securities Held by Foreign Holders

Source: US Treasury Dpt.   WOLFSTREET.com

The data indicate a collective intervention started in October 2022 after UK gilts, Japanese government bonds, and US Treasuries all came under pressure, and banks faced liquidity shortages. The pivot coincided with a G7 treasurers meeting in Washington. Daisy Chains can be stable for quite a long time if carefully managed, but they remain window dressing that avoids tackling the underlying issue of unsustainable fiscal incontinence and debt growth.

Unrealized Gains (Losses) on Investment Securities

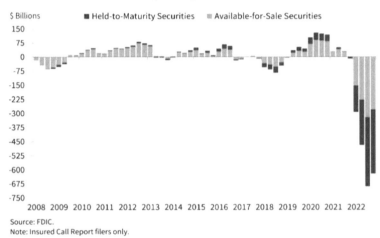

Source: FDIC.
Note: Insured Call Report filers only.

Reforms to market structure policies could help restore market liquidity. Over 400 fixed income markets price against US Treasuries as the 'risk free' rate, which makes UST illiquidity and market dysfunction a global systemic risk. I have long been critical of changes to trade transparency, central counterparty clearing, capital on dealer inventory, and other policies that forced medium and small dealers in USTs from markets and over-concentrated dealing in the top 3 US banks. Unfortunately, it does not appear that any misguided policies will be reviewed or altered, so the rest of the world will need to take measures independently to secure fixed income market stability and improve their own markets' liquidity and capacity. Countries will need to develop resiliency and price determination functions that are independent of a US Treasury market that looks increasingly unstable.

At $307 trillion or so, bonds are the bedrock of the global banking system and write downs impact stability and capacity within banks, insurers, pension funds, and everything connected to them. Write downs on portfolios of sovereign debt are destabilising the Western financial system. Unrealised losses that undercut bank capital have already led to four large bank failures in the US in 2023, and unprecedented central bank intervention that overturns every principle of bank support going back to Bagehot.

The Bank Term Finance Program (BTFP) jointly announced by the Fed and Treasury the weekend Silicon Valley Bank failed is likely an innovation too far. The program buys portfolio bonds of banks needing liquidity at par value for a period of one year. It violates every principle of Bagehot for central bank support in a crisis:

- No policy discrimination between insolvent and illiquid banks;
- No punitive discount to market value to create an incentive favouring market solutions;
- No haircut on the bond collateral to protect the central bank lender.

Worse BTFP creates a two-tier market where banks in the US can borrow at 100% face value while everyone else unfortunate enough to own these same bonds is hit by huge mark downs and collateral haircuts in a less liquid parallel market. Bad policies are metastasising with every new crisis, with no discernible principles, monetary theory, or legal rationale.

Despite these failings, there was no discussion, no challenge, no media engagement on the new programme. It is a measure of how inured we have become to central bank interventions that no one bothers to ask the hard questions about policy rationale and consistency anymore. The group think among policy makers prevents critical enquiry or even objective evaluation of whether policy objectives were achieved and what side effects were observed. Central banks lack accountability as their dependents in government and finance will never challenge them.

The greater challenge is stabilising debt in EMDEs after 75 years of debt-led development. Many EMDE economies, already suffering from the pandemic and global inflation, are facing unsustainable increases in the cost of refinancing or servicing their debts. Their principal creditors are Western financial institutions.

Yasiru @YRanaraja · 02/10/2023

So who owns over $15 billion of Sri Lanka's government debt in the form of sovereign bonds?

Answer: Western Vulture Funds and Banks:

BlackRock (US)
Ashmore Group (Britain)
Allianz (Germany)
UBS (Switzerland)
HSBC (Britain)
JPMorgan Chase (US)
Prudential (US)

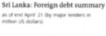

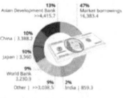

Sri Lanka: Foreign debt summary
as of end April 21 (by major lenders in million US dollars)

81% of Sri Lanka's debt owned by West & Allies not China

Debt distribution and discrimination is not at all equitable. Developing states pay multiples of the interest in advanced economies. According to the UN, 52 countries – almost 40% of EMDEs – have serious debt stress. The burden of servicing debts reduces fiscal capacity for education, health, and internal investment, perpetuating under-development and poverty. The chart below for Latin America and the Caribbean shows debt service larger than education, healthcare, or social provision.

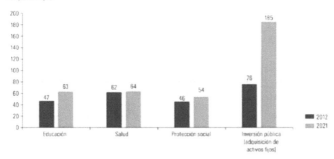

América Latina y el Caribe: relación entre los intereses pagados por el gobierno central y el gasto en educación, atención de salud, protección social e inversión pública, 2012 y 2021
(En porcentajes)

As Western central banks hike rates in line with domestic mandates to control inflation, they escalate the growing debt crisis in the rest of the world. Interest payments are growing more rapidly than other public expenditure. Private creditors, who offer higher rate debt and shorter maturities than multilaterals, are the loan sharks of EMDEs. Private creditors now hold 62% of external public debt, up from 47% a decade ago. Each time debt matures and rolls over it is at higher rates. This is not sustainable.

Debt borrows from future prosperity if used to fund present debt service or consumption rather than investment for future yield. Too much debt has been misallocated, failing to secure future yield. A rethink is long overdue.

THE STATE OF THE WORLD'S DEBT

GOVERNMENT DEBT BY COUNTRY

Debt-to-GDP ratio is a simple metric that compares a country's public debt to its economic output. The higher a country's debt-to-GDP ratio is, the higher the risk for that country defaulting on its debt, therefore creating a financial panic in the markets.

THE DEBT-TO-GDP RATIO 2021 (%)

The World Bank published a study showing that countries with a **debt-to-GDP ratio of 77% or more** during prolonged periods of time cause economic slowdowns.

>250%   >200%   >100%   >77%   >50%

HIGHEST DEBT-TO-GDP

DISCLAIMER

Japan has the highest debt-to-GDP ratio of 257%. In 2010, the country became the first advanced economy to reach 200%.

Countries such as **Venezuela, Afghanistan and Argentina** did not have data available for 2021. All other countries missing are typically not reported on by the IMF, such as North Korea.

*See full sized graphic for detailed country list.

SOURCE: World Economic Outlook Report (October 2021 Edition)

VISUAL CAPITALIST

COLLABORATORS   RESEARCH • WRITING Raul Amoros   ART DIRECTION • DESIGN Harrison Schell, Christina Kostandi

10 TECHNOLOGY AND INFRASTRUCTURE

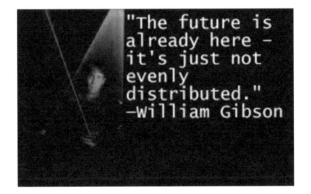

"The future is already here — it's just not evenly distributed."
—William Gibson

Technology is a great leveller of humanity. Before the printing press only elites and clerics were taught to read and write. Now virtually everyone in the world can be literate and communicate through their smart phones. Technology, telecommunications, financial connectivity, and scientific cooperation are globalising at an ever-faster pace. This is good for everyone.

Technology for payments is changing too. Payments technology accelerates the transition from dollar to non-dollar payments for global trade, credit, and digital commerce.

What is a payment? Leaving cash out of it, a payment is an instruction to debit your account on a ledger with a bank, card company, payments provider, or other financial intermediary and credit a payee account on a ledger with the same or another bank or financial intermediary. Whether it is a card payment, online payment, PayPal payment, or Swift message, a payment is instructed via an electronically transmitted structured data message that captures all relevant information about payor, payee, accounts, account-holding intermediaries, currency, value, and transaction reference that is transmitted along the chain of any banks or payment intermediaries between payor and payee.

Structured data is formatted for payments globally through the data standard ISO 20022, one part of the multi-part international standard for financial services. An open standard, anyone can use ISO 20022 to build or modernise their central bank, payment system, or banks. All central banks, banks, and many domestic payment systems have already integrated ISO 20022 into operations or are moving toward ISO 20022 adoption.

Once adoption is complete globally, these systems can be linked for interoperability. Interoperability means that banks outside a domestic payment system can message a payment using a central bank or other clearing platform node on the foreign network.

Payments within a single bank can clear by simple debit and credit across payor and payee accounts, a 'book transfer'. Payments between banks use a domestic payment system linking bank ledgers for debit and credit. National payment systems will continue to dominate payments in their own currencies. Payment systems operating independently outside national borders exist, but are rare.

144

In the past banks wanting to make payment in a currency where they are not direct participants of a domestic payment system used intermediary banks, called nostro banks, to make payment on their behalf. The sending bank funds the nostro bank for the foreign payment in an alternative agreed currency, usually dollar. The nostro intermediation and foreign-exchange funding results in additional costs passed onto the customer. Where a domestic payment can cost micropence, a foreign currency payment through a nostro bank will likely cost much more. The cost of a Swift payment from a UK bank to a foreign bank is typically above £30 ($38).

Banks can profit from intermediating foreign currency payments, charging the fat fee while settling many payments on their own ledgers or at much lower cost. This has led to high concentration in the global banking system. Over decades global payments have consolidated from hundreds of nostro banks down to a few huge global banks. These global banks charge high fees on foreign exchange payments even when they settle a payment on their own ledger between branches of the bank by 'book transfer'.

Citibank, JP Morgan, and Bank of America settle more payments on their internal overnight 'book transfer' than go through the entire Fedwire interbank payment system by a multiple. I explained this to the New York Fed vice president in charge of Fedwire about 20 years ago at a Swift conference. He didn't believe me. We crossed the room together to the head of Citibank payments, who confirmed Citi settled about three times as much in payments overnight as Fedwire on average. It will be more than that now as US payments clearing has continued to concentrate.

This dominance of a few large banks gets challenged if all

banks can join directly to foreign payment systems and transact directly at local costs of micropence through interlinked domestic systems. Many linkages have been announced in the past year, so the global map of payments interlinkages is changing fast. The big banks may resent losing secure income streams, but for globalisation of the world economy the trend is very positive.

Another alternative model is interbank payments clearing owned by cooperating banks and intermediated by clearing banks for each eligible currency. Hong Kong Interbank Clearing Ltd is a private company owned by the Hong Kong Monetary Authority and Hong Kong Association of Banks. HKICL provides real-time interbank payments for member banks in Hong Kong dollar (the domestically issued currency), US dollar, euro, and yuan. HSBC settles HKICL dollar payments by book transfer on its dollar ledger as dollar agent for HKICL. Standard Chartered settles euro payments by book transfer on its euro ledger as euro agent for HKICL. Bank of China (Hong Kong) Ltd settles yuan payments on its ledger as agent of HKICL. The HKICL multicurrency system reduces the costs and delays of settling dollar, euro, and renminbi via nostro banks and interbank systems in distant New York, Frankfurt, and Beijing and can also offer more convenient local operating hours. HKICL provides more cost-effective settlement of foreign exchange transactions in cleared currencies, because HKICL does not need expensive Swift interbank messaging with attendant delays.

Multilateral interoperability among diverse systems may require a supplemental shared platform. One platform that got as far as testing in 2022 was Project mBridge, a collaboration between the BIS Innovation Hub Hong Kong Centre, the Hong Kong Monetary Authority, the Bank of Thailand, the Digital Currency Institute of the

People's Bank of China, and the Central Bank of the United Arab Emirates. Project mBridge uses a custom common platform based on distributed ledger technology (DLT), effectively blockchain, on which central banks issue and exchange central bank digital currencies as tokens. It is a multicurrency CBDC platform that provides exchange of value payment-vs-payment in its eligible currencies, interlinking the inconsistent underlying domestic platforms.

The mBridge ledger supports real-time peer-to-peer cross-border payments and foreign exchange transactions in compliance with jurisdiction of issue policies and legal requirements. The platform is not ready for commercial operations at scale, however, as additional work is required on supplemental liquidity, compliance, and connectivity, as well as agreement on a common legal and governance framework.

They could save a lot of time and effort by simply expanding the HKICL model already fully in operation to Thai bhat and UAE dirham and opening HKICL to cooperating banks in each jurisdiction. Block chain ledgers have no satisfactory use cases in reduced complexity and costs two decades after publication of the Bitcoin algorithm. Additionally, security has been repeatedly compromised within the sphere of digital assets and exchanges, with some of the biggest frauds and hacks in history revealed in recent years, often directed by management or insiders. Finally, payment-vs-payment transactions have never been used by banks or corporations in any commercial context, and none have the accounting or operating systems for mBridge functions. An earlier payment-vs-payment commercial platform founded by a successful payments entrepreneur called RTGS.Global is still looking for commercial use case five years later.

There is no need for central orchestration or standardisation by the BIS or Swift for domestic and foreign payments systems to be made interoperable. More likely, central orchestration will be unwelcome and suspect. Swift has an unfortunate track record of making messaging data available to US intelligence authorities. The BIS is not trusted as neutral in its policies and operations by many central banks in the global East and South. Despite its name, the BIS has no track record in modern multilateral payments and settlements at scale.

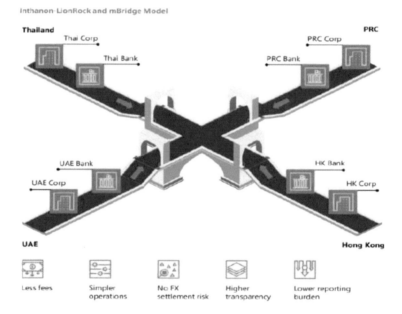

Inthanon-LionRock and mBridge Model

National and commercial diversity and optionality in international payments is a good thing. It allows comparison and innovation to drive efficiency and new services. Competition lets us evaluate what works and what is most cost-effective, but not without regulation and supervision. Too many innovative platforms have been poorly managed and fraud-prone. Banks remain useful as payments intermediaries, but PayPal, Wise, AliPay, and WeChat Pay have demonstrated scope for intermediation and agility in globalised payment operations.

10 BETTER IS POSSIBLE

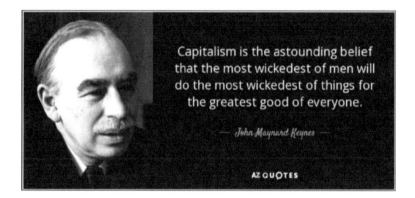

Capitalism is the astounding belief that the most wickedest of men will do the most wickedest of things for the greatest good of everyone.

— John Maynard Keynes —

AZ QUOTES

The purpose of monetary and economic policies should be to support the wellbeing of the citizenry. Somewhere along the way the monetary and economic policies were hijacked to serve the interests of a very few. If the world now choses to experiment with different monetary and economic policies, we should welcome the experimentation. Diversity invites comparison, and from that we learn what works better and furthers public interests.

We shouldn't mourn the gradual passing of the unipolar dollar as Multicurrency Mercantilism emerges. The unipolar dollar world was violent, unjust, divisive, corrupt, exploitative, and unfair to most humans on this planet, even in Western economies. It is too early to say whether the multipolar world now emerging will be safer, more just, unifying, equitable, accountable, and fair, but we can

When plunder becomes a way of life for a group of men in a society, over the course of time they create for themselves a legal system **that authorizes it** and a moral code **that glorifies it.**

Frederic Bastiat

individually, nationally, and collectively work to achieve better, measure the outcomes, and hold institutions and leadership accountable.

BRICS+, ASEAN, and other organisations embracing a shift to Local Currency Trade encourage multilateral and bilateral cooperation for security, long-term growth, and shared prosperity. It's rational to let them get on with it, watch the data, and see if they are onto a winning method.

The failure of 20th century multilateral institutions is that they did not deter the strong from brutalising or impoverishing the weak, nor did they curb bad political and monetary policies, in either rich or poor states. We have wasted decades, but we start from where we are with successful models of Singapore, China, Vietnam, United Arab Emirates, Luxembourg, and other states with stable growth and good governance. From here each state chooses a model suiting their own circumstances and adapts it, learning from experience. States, banks, and institutions might even experiment with multiple interlinkages and models to evaluate and compare outcomes.

All of us are more alike than we are different, and most of us want the same things. When asked what makes life meaningful, no one answers 'democracy' or 'values'. These words are media weapons to shape conflict and division.

Whenever I hear about Western 'democracy', 'values', or a 'rules based order' I now ask why do they want me to believe the narrative they are spinning? It rings an inner alarm. It is better to look at objective data on longevity, employment, household formation, healthcare, environmental changes, education and other measurable attributes to judge whether political systems meet the aspirations of their citizens. The more objective we become in holding governments to account, the more likely they are to serve the public rather than elites.

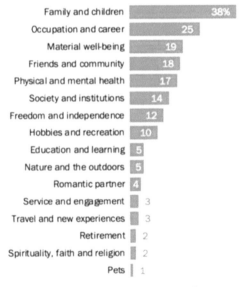

Family, careers and material well-being are among the most cited factors for what makes life meaningful

Median % who mention ___ when describing what gives them meaning in life

Family and children	38%
Occupation and career	25
Material well-being	19
Friends and community	18
Physical and mental health	17
Society and institutions	14
Freedom and independence	12
Hobbies and recreation	10
Education and learning	5
Nature and the outdoors	5
Romantic partner	4
Service and engagement	3
Travel and new experiences	3
Retirement	2
Spirituality, faith and religion	2
Pets	1

Note: Percentages are medians based on 17 publics. Open-ended question. See Appendix A for more information.
Source: Spring 2021 Global Attitudes Survey. Q36.
"What Makes Life Meaningful? Views from 17 Advanced Economies"

PEW RESEARCH CENTER

Even small states can be inspirational. El Salvador was plagued by violent gangs for decades. Murders peaked in 2015 at 6,665. President Nayib Bukele achieved a full year elapsing to 11 May 2023 with zero murders. It is a spectacular success story of full spectrum enforcement against violent crime. While not endorsing every aspect of the gang incarceration policy, President Bukele has achieved something of a public policy and economic miracle for his nation. He has since used his popularity to push for streamlined regional governments and reduced corruption. This year Google chose El Salvador for its Central American base and Cloud and digital expansion plans.

Nayib Bukele ✓
@nayibbukele

Cerramos el 10 de mayo de 2023, con 0 homicidios a nivel nacional.

Con este, son 365 días sin homicidios, todo un año.
Translate post

365 días
sin homicidios

0:06 / 1:31

7:53 AM · May 11, 2023 · **6.9M** Views

The Belt and Road Initiative, now entering its 10th year, drove infrastructure-first development methods in cooperating economies. The results are impressive. Much of the infrastructure is grant financed, without debt. If these countries now grow faster, outperforming peer states that did not cooperate in BRI, it is evidence that better is not only possible, better was delivered.

Jason Smith - 上官杰文 ✔ @ShangguanJiewen · 2h
Replying to @USAmbJapan

3/4 of the world are members of the #beltandroad. It has built power plants, schools, bridges, hospitals, universities and more.

History will remember the BRI as a turning point, when the developing world turned the tables on the former imperialists.

x.com/ShangguanJiewe...

> ⬤ **Jason Smith - 上官杰文** ✔ @ShangguanJiewen · 22h
> China built an $82 million powerplant for #Burundi, free.
>
> Opening in 2022, the 15MW Ruzibazi Power Plant provides 1/3 of electricity in Burundi. It includes a water diversion system, powerhouses, a booster station & transmission lines.
>
> #BeltandRoad
> china.aiddata.org/projects/57106/.

Studying the BRICS+ model from the outside, it seems to work by identifying a national need and matching it with another state or non-state actor's existing outperformance, capacity, and willingness to invest. For example, India lacks supercontainer ports fitted with modern AI port logistics automation. DP World has a network of ports throughout the world and the capacity to identify best practice from all its global port operations. In the wake of the BRICS XV Summit, DP World announced $510 million investment deal with Deendayal Port Authority to build, operate, and maintain a new container terminal near Kandla Port in the state of Gujarat. India gets improved global export capacity to modern standards of AI-assisted speed and efficiency, and DP World gets another port on its network as a mature and trusted operator. India should attract more investment in export industrialisation, fixing a current weakness.

Collaborative development that extends proven capacity and management to expand capacity where it is needed is a big improvement on multilateral lending with no local accountability and conditionality unsuited to local capacity building. Good governance is learned by observing, studying, and modelling good governance. Peer to peer collaboration will build capacity with greater credibility.

Tanzania Business Insight ⏀
@TanzaniaInsight

DP WORLD SIGNS AGREEMENT TO DEVELOP $510 MILLION CONTAINER TERMINAL IN INDIA

Dubai-owned ports giant DP World will invest around $510 million to build a new container terminal at the Kandla port in the Indian state of Gujarat, its group chairman said on Friday.

"It will enable the delivery of trade opportunities by connecting northern, western and central India with global markets," Sultan Ahmed Bin Sulayem, who is also DP World's CEO, said after the signing of an agreement between the Deendayal Port Authority and DP World officials.

- Reuters

Last edited 8:01 PM · Aug 25, 2023 · 11.5K Views

18 Reposts   3 Quotes   50 Likes   2 Bookmarks

Note the Tweet I've used is from Tanzania. In this world of immediately shared information and news, other countries can see progress and prepare for similar engagement. The BRICS+ model could scale globally without materially challenging Western capital markets because it happens at the margins, bilaterally, in markets largely excluded from Western finance. Again, if we see faster growth and more equitable development in BRICS+ economies, we have proof that better is possible because better has been delivered.

I standardised securities and derivatives laws globally and built some of the architecture of the dollarised world. I'm proud that my work grew bigger global financial markets and spread best practice. A similar effort will be required to integrate all currencies and commercial norms for safer, more equitable trading and finance, but the potential benefits are huge.

I'm committed to that work, and so are the Team at Pacemaker.Global, with whoever will work with us.

"The secret of change is to focus all of your energy not on fighting the old, but on building the new."

SOCRATES

Per Capita GDP Growth Lived Change Index

The index uses lifetime per capita GDP to track how much economic change a population has experienced. Over the past three decades China has changed more quickly than any other place on earth.

Per capita GDP growth in the top 40 global economies, 1990–2019

source: Harvard Business Review
source: World Bank

ABOUT THE AUTHOR

Kathleen Tyson started at the Federal Reserve Bank of New York with responsibility for derivatives, securities, and systemic risk. She was recruited to the UK Securities and Investments Board to supervise international markets and global settlements at Euroclear and Clearstream. At Clearstream she co-invented Triparty Repo, optimised bilateral derivatives margin, and got US Treasuries, bonds and equities into Luxembourg. Founding a consultancy, she then built CLS Bank foreign exchange settlements with IBM, designed supervision, governance and operations of NASDAQ Dubai, modernised exchange traded derivatives clearing at LCH-Clearnet, and standardised a fully modern, integrated operating platform to 14 central banks with Intellect. As founder and chief executive of Pacemaker.Global, she will provide secured interbank liquidity in all currencies for the Multipolar and Multicurrency integrated global economy.

Made in United States
Troutdale, OR
12/15/2024

26361148R00093